POWER PERSONAL BRANDS

A HANDS-ON GUIDE
TO
UNDERSTANDING YOURS

BY
BEN BAKER

POWERFUL PERSONAL BRANDS:
A Hands-On Guide to Understanding Yours

Copyright © 2018 Ben Baker

Cover Designer: Ana Chabrand, Chabrand Design House
www.anachabrand.com
Back Cover Photo: Kent Kallberg
www.kentkallberg.com
Interior Formatting: Iryna Spica
www.spicabookdesign.com

ISBNs:
978-1-77374-030-0 (print)
978-1-77374-031-7 (eBook)

Your Brand Marketing,
A Division of CMYK Solutions, Inc.
Richmond, BC
Canada
www.yourbrandmarketing.com

This book belongs to:

_____

I define my Powerful Personal Brand as:

_____

_____

_____

_____

_____

_____

_____

_____

Thank you for purchasing a copy of my book.
As a thank you, here is a gift
A Coupon Code: PowerfulPersonalBrands
This is a $50.00 discount on a set of 4 x 1 hour online
personal brand consulting sessions
Yes, that means you are getting this book for FREE!
Please go to:
https://yourbrandmarketing.com/consulting/#personal

I believe that your POWERFUL PERSONAL BRAND defines who you are today and gives you the tools to become who you wish to be.
Your POWERFUL PERSONAL BRAND allows you to have the confidence to achieve great things.
It is the framework that allows you to close bigger sales, lead teams more effectively, or run larger organizations more successfully.
In other words, it is the key to maximizing your ongoing success!

– Ben Baker

DEDICATIONS

I want to thank everyone who helped me make this book possible. No one does anything alone and it is only with support, motivation, and advice from others that things get done.

Writing this book was a process and those who helped me are appreciated:

Editors: Jae M. Rang, Joan Ouchi, Tara Hartley
Susan Rooks – www.grammargoddess.com,
Book production: Cascadia Author Services –
www.cascadiaauthorservices.com
Publisher: Your Brand Marketing –
www.yourbrandmarketing.com
Contributors: Anthony C. Taylor, Garry Priam, Jae M. Rang, John White, Lisa Dawson, Lucia Fuenmayor, Mark Fidelman, Pat Kalehan, Phill Domask, Shawn Hall, Stephanie Koonar and Tim McClure
Friends and Family: Anastasia, Andrea, Christopher, Glenda, Heather, Robbie, Seth and Stan.

I appreciate your support and advice more than you will ever know.

TABLE OF CONTENTS

FOREWORD. xi

1   Whose POWERFUL PERSONAL BRAND has
Influenced Me?. 1

2   *John White, Founder Social Media Solutions* 7

3   In the Beginning. 9

4   Then We Went to School 15

5   *Stephanie Koonar, Marketing Instructor Langara
School Of Management* 21

6   Growing Up in the Age of Social Media 23

7   *Anthony C Taylor, Managing Partner And Lead
Facilitator Sme Strategy* 35

8   Now the Process Begins 39

9   *Lisa Dawson, President Ljd Management*. 43

10   What are Three Experiences from Your Youth
that Made You what You are Today . . .
And Why? 47

11 Who are the Top Three People You Admire . . .
    And Why? 55

12 *Lucia Fuenmayor, Channel Manager*
    Quick Mobile 63

13 What are the Three Most Important Things
    in Your Life . . . And Why? 65

14 What are Three Ideals or Beliefs You Hold
    Above Others . . . And Why?. 71

15 *Shawn Hall, President Apogee Public Relations* . . 77

16 What were Three Work Experiences that
    Helped Shape You . . . And Why? 79

17 What are Your Three Favourite Songs or
    Movies . . . And Why? 87

18 *Garry Priam, President Mossa International* 93

19 What are Three Experiences From Your
    Adult Life that You will Never Forget . . .
    And Why? 95

20 So, what Happens when Things Go Wrong?. . 103

21 What are You Passionate About . . .
    And Why? 105

22 *Phill Domask, President The Phill Domask*
    Consultancy 111

23 How do You Volunteer . . . And Why do You Do It? 115

24 The Power of a Personal Manifesto 119

25 *Mark Fidelman, President Fanatics Media* 127

26 You Cannot Fake Authenticity 129

27 Creating a Concise Personal Vision Statement 133

28 *Patrick Kelahan, Forensic Market Strategist H2m Architects And Engineers* 139

29 Personality Tests You May Want to Consider 141

30 So, Who are You? 145

31 *Jae M. Rang, President Jae Associated Ltd.* 149

32 Now Here are Some Tips on How to Apply what You Have Learned. 153

33 Always Have a Story to Tell. 161

34 *Tim McClure, President Tim McClure and Partners.* 167

35 So, Now What? 173

36 *Ben Baker, President Your Brand Marketing.* ... 175

Epilogue 179

About the Author. 183

FOREWORD

The reason I wrote this book is my overwhelming belief that each one of us has something that makes us unique and special in this world – the Power of Your Personal Brand.

In this book, I will refer to "I," "you," "he," "she," "they," and "us," but I realize that the pronoun does not matter as we are all on this journey together. We all live in a world of 525,600 minutes (nod to the musical "RENT") in a year, and we all are hurtling around the sun at the same speed.

We may be rich, poor, a different colour, a different ethnicity, and have different beliefs, but we all come from one race, and that is the human race.

Through this book, I am asking you to take the time to really think about this: No one is better and no one is worse; we are just different in how we perceive things based upon what brought us to this point in time and space.

Embrace your differences and your uniqueness. Take the time to understand what things you believe and why. How did you get to where you are and where are you going? We all have our own journey, and the more we can embrace it, celebrate it, and communicate what we believe, the more interesting we can be to others we encounter along the way.

Note: This book is not a self-help, hug-each-other and run-for-your-therapist type of book. It is based upon my reality and the realities of hundreds of people who I know and have spoken to from around the world. Each of us has had different experiences and will continue to. Instead, this is a workbook designed to help you think about who you were, who you are, and who you would like to be.

The purpose of this book is for you to realize that no matter where you came from, it is up to you to help determine your future. You are no better, or worse, than anyone else out there. All you have is a different set of experiences that have brought you to where you are. Celebrate your individuality, understand what makes you special, and communicate it in ways so that others will listen, understand, internalize, and engage.

DEFINING WHY...

In Simon Sinek's famous book *Start With Why*, he asks us to put aside the what and the how and focus first on why we want to achieve what we want to achieve. In this book, the why is to help you understand your POWERFUL PERSONAL BRAND and communicate it, so that others will listen, understand, engage, and see value in your brand. I believe that only through others understanding the value of your brand can you develop trust and spread influence. In my opinion, influence and trust are the cornerstones to achieving personal success. Whether it is getting that first job, convincing someone to marry you, getting a promotion, closing a big deal, leading a team or a company, or just having your opinion matter in everyday life, your POWERFUL PERSONAL BRAND unlocks your success.

POWERFUL PERSONAL BRANDS

A HANDS-ON GUIDE
TO
UNDERSTANDING YOURS

CHAPTER ONE

WHOSE POWERFUL PERSONAL BRAND HAS INFLUENCED ME?

There are many who have influenced my thoughts over the years and have given me tools that have allowed me to be who I am, but I want to tell you a story of a particular POWERFUL PERSONAL BRAND in my life that has not only influenced me, and this book, but has inspired millions of people around the world.

SETH GODIN

Seth Godin has been inspiring and influencing me as a marketer for as long as I can remember. He is an inductee into the Marketing Hall of Fame and the author of more books than I could list. It is his writing, which has been my window into his soul and how he has spread his influence in a consistent and deliberate manner. To date, he has written over 7000 daily blog posts and numerous books, developed courses, and spoken publicly with one single thought in mind. That thought is, to paraphrase; it is up to all of us to make a ruckus. Each of us needs to do work that matters and ship work that we are proud of. Each of us has something that we can contribute to making the world we live in just a little bit better, and we must do so.

In the spring of 2017, I was fortunate enough to see a blog post from Seth Godin advertising a new program he was calling "The Marketing Seminar". There were very few details about what the program was about, but I knew it would be fifty videos in one hundred days, and an opportunity to have discussions on the subjects with people from around the globe. This was enough impetus for me to sign on the dotted line. True to Seth's word, every few days another video would appear asking us to think differently on a variety of marketing subjects and then provided a space online for discourse. In this original class, there were about eighteen hundred of us. In the beginning, we all floundered, trying to understand the subjects at a deeper level and to discuss the topics intelligently. Within a few weeks, there was clearly a separation between those who decided to sit back and watch and listen and those who rolled up their sleeves, dug in, and challenged each other to do better. What I did not realize was that my true personality was coming out.

I learn best by teaching others. By taking the time to read other people's thoughts and discuss ideas openly and honestly, I was learning far more than just answering the questions Seth posed. What I also did not realize was that the software we were using kept track of our actions and even though we did not realize it, Seth was watching it all.

One day, I was out for coffee, and my phone started ringing; the caller display said, Seth Godin. I had no idea who had spoofed the number or who was playing a trick on me, but I answered the phone anyway. On the other end of the phone, I heard, "Hi, it's Seth, I like what you have been doing in the seminar, and I would like you to come and be an adjunct teacher for our accelerated summer session." I am not sure those were the exact words, but they are pretty close. I was blown over, I was excited, and I immediately said, "Yes."

I asked what this encompassed and what Seth said was just to keep doing what I had been doing and keep the conversations going.

This was a wonderful three months of my life. The seminar was supposed to go a month, but they kept the dialogue open longer to allow people to catch up, and I did not care. The opportunity to tap into the ideas and thoughts of so many people and learn from them, while helping guide conversations, was unbelievable.

WHAT DID I LEARN FROM THIS?

- First and foremost was that I had a voice and ideas of value. I always thought so before, but this experience gave me the confidence to take my thinking to the next level.

- That I enjoy teaching and with that, I have refocused my business so that all I do is consult, provide workshops, and speak on brand, message, market, vision, and value.

- That perfect is an ideal that none of us can afford. We need to be constantly innovating, shipping good work out the door, evaluating it, and then working to make it better. If we wait until something is perfect before we launch it, nothing will ever get launched.

- People like us do things like this. It is a mantra of Seth's. What does it mean? It means that we cannot please everyone and not everyone will be our client. Find those whose problems you understand and can solve and communicate with them. They are your tribe, and they will be loyal because they know you are working with their best interest at heart.

- Be authentic. If you cannot be true to your ideals, you are nothing; trying to be something you are not does not help anyone.

- Creativity is the true key to success. Having the desire to look at problems differently, being open to new ideas and new solutions, and being willing to fail is what will help you succeed in the end.

I will always be grateful to Seth for the lessons learned and the experience gained. It has helped make me a better person and has allowed me to provide my clients with more value.

THOUGHTS FROM VARIOUS LEADERS ON POWERFUL PERSONAL BRANDS

As part of writing this book, I felt compelled to have opinions outside of my own. Experience has shown that by taking the best of the advice of others, and meshing it with your own beliefs, you form opinions that are stronger and more informed.

With that, I asked people I know from across North America, with different experiences, different viewpoints, and different philosophies, to add their voices to this project and provide insights from their own experience. Their answers will be strategically placed throughout this book.

WHAT I ASKED THEM TO DO IS PONDER A SERIES OF QUESTIONS:

1. What is your definition of a POWERFUL PERSONAL BRAND?

2. How has your POWERFUL PERSONAL BRAND allowed you to gain success in your industry?

3. What advice would you give to those looking to create their own POWERFUL PERSONAL BRAND?

4. How do you perceive having a POWERFUL PERSONAL BRAND helps someone either secure a job or advance within a company?

Not everyone answered all four questions, and no one's answers are either right or wrong. They are merely their opinions based upon their experiences. Take them as a collective, something to be viewed in aggregate and learned from as a body of work. Some of them will resonate with you, and some will not. That is okay. It is incorporating the information in this book with your own experiences and finding ways to understand why you do what you do that is important.

Once you have read them all, take the time to answer these questions yourself. Understand what you agree with, what you do not, and why. How do the opinions of these people help shape your POWERFUL PERSONAL BRAND, and how do you feel you can best communicate your value in ways that others will want to engage with?

NOTE: *In honouring those who have responded to these questions, I have not altered their words in any way, and they remain the words and opinions of the contributors.*

CHAPTER TWO

JOHN WHITE
FOUNDER
SOCIAL MEDIA SOLUTIONS

1. **What is your definition of a POWERFUL PERSONAL BRAND?**

   A POWERFUL PERSONAL BRAND creates inbound opportunities for people due to their high level of influence within their niche.

2. **How has your POWERFUL PERSONAL BRAND allowed you to gain success in your industry?**

   Prior to my having a personal brand, I was always the one doing the pitching. I made cold job submissions on the web. I made cold calls. I begged people in senior level positions to give me the time of day.

   That all changed four years ago when I completed an MBA, went viral a few times on LinkedIn, and opened Social Marketing Solutions.

After investing heavily in my personal brand, I'm not always having to be the one pitching others. Now, opportunities seem to find me organically.

3. **What advice would you give to those looking to create their own POWERFUL PERSONAL BRAND?**

I would tell them to be prolific with their networking efforts. Don't sit back and wait for people to find you. Building a personal brand requires you to have an active network around you.

Be genuine in your outreach, and send personalized messages and you will be amazed at who you connect with.

4. **How do you perceive having a POWERFUL PERSONAL BRAND helps someone either secure a job or advance within a company?**

The first thing a POWERFUL PERSONAL BRAND does is that it helps recruiters find you because when they do keyword searches, you appear higher in the rankings than someone with a limited personal brand.

It also gives you credibility and authority that can separate you from the others in a field of applicants. Writing a book, running a podcast, building an engaged following on social media, blogging, creating videos, and speaking at events are all examples of ways that you can build a POWERFUL PERSONAL BRAND that helps you stand out from the pack of applicants.

CHAPTER THREE

IN THE BEGINNING . . .

THE FIRST SIX YEARS

"The first six years of a child's life are important to their development and future education. Children who are cared for and have positive experiences during the early years are more likely to develop and learn in ways that help them meet their full potential.

Lifelong learning begins the moment we are born. The first six years of our lives are a time of unparalleled discovery. We learn about ourselves and the world around us. Our personalities take shape, and we begin to lay the foundation of knowledge that will support us as we enter the education system."

Alberta Education https://education.alberta.ca/ early-childhood-education/childhood-development/

In the beginning, we are all the same. We all come into this world without knowledge or understanding of race, religion, economic power, or prestige. As little children, we played happily, and sometimes not so much, with all the other kids around us.

We learned that it was good to share, to play nice with others, and to say please and thank you. We also learned the subtle ways to get what we wanted, whether our parents wanted to give in or not. We learned about consequences and that sometimes we do not win. We also learned a new word . . . FAIR, and we learned through experience what was and what was not fair.

This was a time when we were totally dependent on others. We could not fend for ourselves, articulate our hopes, needs, and desires in a meaningful way, and even if we could have, we might not have been listened to as much as we would have liked. We had to rely on those bigger than we were for food, drink, comfort, warmth, love, and advice. Sometimes we were grateful, sometimes we were not, but we were always learning. Our parents were the most important people in our lives, and for the most part, they tried their best, without a manual or a video to watch, to teach us, to take care of us, and to encourage us along the way.

However, what our parents did not fully understand at the time was how intently we were watching them. How every action they took, every lesson they taught, and every word they said was taken in, analyzed, processed, and mimicked. As children, we did learn through playing and engaging with the other kids, but also from how our parents' interactions imprinted upon us as we grew up. We learned at a young age that it is not as much what people say that matters, it's the actions that go along with those words that truly create meaning in our lives.

How many times have you heard parents say "NO" to a child and then five minutes later give in and give the child exactly what they want anyway? How many times have we told our kids to always wear a helmet when riding a bike, but we do not wear ours when we are out riding with them? How many times do we tell kids not to yell in the house, and then have a heated argument with our spouse that they can hear? It is not so much what people tell us that we remember; it is what they show us through their actions that make the big difference. This leads me to think that no matter your age and no matter who you are speaking with, it is critical to remember that words, if not backed up with consistent action, will tear into the fabric of your personal brand.

Not only did we learn that actions are more important than words at a young and impressionable age, but we learned about status. Status, under the age of six, is an interesting thing. In my opinion, it is not measured through your actions; it is measured through your interactions. Have you ever noticed how certain kids' moms have cooler strollers than others, nicer diaper bags, and bigger cars? How well some kids are dressed, no matter where they are, and how some are not? How some kids have the coolest and greatest toys, and others don't?

Well, none of this is by accident. It is a game of status that has played out for as long as there have been parents and children. Every new parent, or at least the vast majority, is drawn into the buying craze that comes with a newborn child. A younger version of myself once referred to it as "the luggage years," the time from age 0-5 where the house, car, grandparents' home, daycare, or wherever is just filled with stuff. Strollers, playpens, bottles, sippy cups, toys, puzzles, building blocks, tricycles, and clothes . . . O M G . . . the clothes. We, as parents, feel that by not having everything constantly within our child's reach, we are somehow depriving them; we need to have every opportunity known to mankind at their fingertips or else they will not grow up healthy and happy.

But, what is this teaching kids? By giving them everything they want, before they even know that they want it, no value is attached to any of it. It becomes the expected and the norm, and when they do not have something that someone else has, they feel that they have been short-changed and are hard-done-by. A child who has everything cannot discern what a want is, what a need is, what is important, and what is not. Think about this from your adult point of view. How much of all of our self-worth is tied up in material things? And even when we get them, we are not happy. We just start looking for the next thing in our lives to purchase. It comes from our childhood, a learned response, and one that we need to unlearn to build a strong personal brand. We need to learn to be happy with who we are and not with what we have!

Not only are the things that you received or did not receive as a child imprinted on who you are today, but so are the interactions you had with people from an early age. The people who were around you, from the time you were very young, helped make you who you are today. An easy example of this is grandparents. I grew up without them. Three out of four of them were not alive on my first birthday, and my father's mother lived thousands of miles away so I barely saw her. My wife, on the other hand, grew up with her mother's parents always around her, and they had a strong familial bond. I am not saying that one is magically better than the other, but I am saying is that by either having grandparents or not, we both had very different types of childhoods and, as a result, different memories.

Another example of how status plays a part in determining our brand, which is extremely obvious, is the neighbourhood park in the middle of the day. Have you ever gone for a walk and noticed how some kids looked just like the people they were with, and some did not look anything like the women who were taking care of them? Hmmm, I wonder what that means? Nannies, au pairs, and the like are a reality in today's world as they have been for decades, if not centuries. With the cost of living today, an increasing number of parents require dual incomes and need to rely on others' help to raise children so that the family can make ends meet. Some families are lucky enough to be able to rely on grandparents; however, others must rely on wonderful daycare, nannies, or au pairs to take care of the children during working hours.

Again, I am not saying any of this to cause angst or anxiety; it is merely a fact of life and whatever way a child is raised, or by whom, forces a child to grow up in a certain way based upon the people who they were around and the experiences they had. No one experience or childhood is inherently better than another, but each different childhood creates the foundation of who a child becomes and what their personal brand will be.

In the end, we all played together, and at least in the early stages, we were blissfully unaware of status and everything that came with it. What we need to realize, though, is that every experience we have, both good and bad, helps make up who we are and that is the brand we showcase to the world. Embracing our good, bad, and ugly, and learning from all of it will help us build a personal brand that helps us achieve our goals in life.

CHAPTER FOUR

THEN *WE WENT* TO SCHOOL . . .

School has been stated over and over again to be little more than a social experiment. It does not matter if you are rich or poor, went to a public or private school, or had good teachers or bad. This is where we all learned to either love or hate ourselves and formed an opinion of who we are based upon our own beliefs and the beliefs of others.

What is most important in the sentence above is the thought process that our personal brand, who we are at the core, is determined as much by others as it is by us. How people perceive you and the value that they place on you, based upon their own sets of ideas and ideals, has as much to do with your brand, as a whole, as your beliefs about yourself.

Again, you are responsible for your own self. The thoughts, ideas, actions, wants, needs, and feelings that you put out in the world influence how people feel about you and whether they believe in you and trust you. If you are known for being a liar and a cheat, that is your brand, no matter how much you protest. Actions will always speak louder than words. People are perceptive, and if there is something about you that they just do not trust, they will not trust you. That is why you need to be who you are. Trying to be what you are not, or worse, trying to be someone else, is artificial. People will pick up on it, call it for what it is, and marginalize those who are not authentic.

In school, it is tough. Everyone wants to be liked and everyone wants to be the popular girl or boy, but the sad point is, not everyone can. There are the "nerds," "geeks," "jocks," "cheerleaders," "drama queens," and "stoners," and then there is everyone else who are just trying to get by. It is not an easy place to be. Whether it is elementary, middle school, or high school, society is placing a lot of pressure on every student to "fit in" and "be part of the system." But as kids, what does that mean?

Some kids have parents who have no time for them, and some kids have parents who never leave them alone. Some kids have parents who never look at grade point averages and want to know what the kids are learning, and some kids have parents think you're not trying if you get 95% on a math test. So, how do you figure out where you belong when you have all this competing noise happening inside your head? How do you find your place in the world, when the world that you live in is constantly telling you that you need to fit into a set of confines that do not make sense to you?

I am here to say that there is no easy answer for this. The best thing I can tell anyone is that school is about experimentation. It is probably the safest place you can be to break out of your comfort zone and try new things. It may not seem like it at the time, but this is where you can dye your hair purple and wear a nose ring, and no one is going to fire you. You can experiment with different types of music, ideas, and thought processes, and the mistakes you make, within the safety of the school years, will be relatively minor. It is a great place to experiment, figure out what you like, what you dislike, what your values are, and what they are not. It is a great place to understand what is important to you and why. It is where you can find your voice if you are brave enough to, and live a life that is slightly uncomfortable and scary.

School is a time to ask WHY and search for answers! It is far more than the "A" that you received on the paper; it is what you learned about yourself on your way to getting the "A." How do you act under pressure? How do you work well, or do you, with others? Are you a leader or a follower? Do you have strong opinions, and are you willing to voice them? School is a place where you can fall down, make a mess, fail, and learn from each and all of these things and figure out how to do it better next time.

As you get older, failure becomes scarier and more risky. It does not mean you should stop testing the limits . . . you shouldn't . . . but when you were in school, you had the luxury of time and a safety net. Hopefully, you used both to their full advantage.

WHO IS YOUR AUDIENCE?

Learn from those around you . . . every day! Watch how people interact and engage. Sometimes people are courteous and act with respect, and sometimes they do not. Learn from both! Understand why you appreciate the actions of certain people and not others. Understand WHY you like certain people and not others. Internalize the qualities you respect in other people and incorporate their mannerisms into your own. Never copy one person, but take a bit from everyone and mix it into your own belief structure to develop a brand that is yours and yours alone.

Everyone will teach you something, even if it is the thing you never want to be known for. It is up to you to watch, listen, understand, internalize, and learn. The more people you watch, the more you will learn about who you want to be and who you do not want to be. Take it all in, process it, make it yours, and verbalize it.

Everything I am telling you to do is easy to say and hard to do, no matter what age you are. But, it is work you need to do to be able to create a personal brand. A personal brand is who you are, what you believe, and why you believe it. It is also how others perceive you and why they find you valuable.

Your brand is unique to you, and your message needs to be as well. This is why I have dwelled on your youth for the last two chapters. Not because I want to put you into psychotherapy or give you a reason to hate your parents, but for you to understand that you ARE a culmination of the experiences that have brought you to this point in your life. Embrace all of them, relate back to them, understand what they have taught you, and figure out how they have made you the person that you are today.

CHAPTER FIVE

STEPHANIE KOONAR
MARKETING INSTRUCTOR
LANGARA SCHOOL OF MANAGEMENT

1. **What is your definition of a POWERFUL PERSONAL BRAND?**

   Your brand is your essence. It is what you innately bring to your relationships, tasks, roles, and duties. It is how you show up in the world. Think of those times when you felt energized and others around you felt energized and you felt like you were in the flow, operating at a high level of performance. It is times like this that you are operating from your essence or your strengths and this is powerful.

2. **How has your POWERFUL PERSONAL BRAND allowed you to gain success in your industry?**

   By being aware of what I contribute and what I can bring to my team or to a project has allowed me to be more successful and contribute to the success of others. My strengths are I tend to bring enthusiasm, energy, and positivity to a team. I also enjoy being part of a team where we are all aligned with a clear goal or purpose. One of my strengths is that I require clarity around team goals and objectives and using my communication strengths I can facilitate clarifying the team goal. So by showing up where I can use and bring these strengths, I operate at my best and I am most successful.

3. **What advice would you give to those looking to create their own POWERFUL PERSONAL BRAND?**

   I believe having a keen understanding of self is key. I highly recommend asking for feedback and looking to assessments like StrengthsFinder to help you understand your strengths and what you contribute. Also, it is key to understand what aren't your strengths or blind spots so that you can work with others "interdependently" where they can cover off your blind spots.

4. **How do you perceive having a POWERFUL PERSONAL BRAND helps someone either secure a job or advance within a company?**

   Being able to articulate your personal brand will enhance your ability to seek out the conditions or environments where you can bring your strengths and contribute. Being able to share how you will contribute will help others to see how you might fit in at their organization or in a new role at your current company.

CHAPTER SIX

GROWING UP IN THE AGE OF SOCIAL MEDIA . . .

Let me start this chapter by saying that I am going to leave the justification of why people do what they do to others. The psychological underpinnings of what we do and to whom are better left to people much more versed in this than I am. I want to focus on what is, or at least what is from a point of view based upon my experiences. What is important to acknowledge and internalize is that everything here is written from one person's point of view. It does not make it right for everyone; it is just an interpretation, based upon what I have observed and the world view that has brought me to this point and time.

We all live in a digital world. We cannot help it if we live in what's known as the "First World," and everyone else is desperately trying to catch up. We all love the conveniences that technology brings and how it allows us freedom that we would not have enjoyed 50 years or even 20 years ago. Technology has been, is, and will be advancing at a pace incomprehensible by most, but it is the result of technological innovation that has brought us to where we are today.

THE TRICK WITH THE DIGITAL WORLD IS TO GET IT TO WORK FOR YOU AND NOT THE OTHER WAY AROUND!

Today, digital encompasses everything from how we access information to how we communicate. All of this, in one way or another, shapes our personal brand.

When we think digital, most people think social media and all the permutations of this. Social media is how we gather information, it is our window into relationships, and it is how we communicate. How we use social media influences how we perceive ourselves and how others perceive us.

Social media, in terms of personal brand building, can be seen to give a nod to Clint Eastwood in *The Good, the Bad and the Ugly*. It influences our brands and shapes them in ways that we may not realize or understand. It can allow us to have a positive or negative voice and can either prop up our personal brand or destroy it. The issue is that most of us are using a tool in social media that we do not truly understand how to use effectively. Like any other tool, it can be used for good, or if people are careless, it can hurt and maim. The more aware we are of who we are, what we believe, who our audience is, how we communicate with them and why, the more effectively we can build a personal brand others will be attracted to, want to engage with, and promote.

WHY NOT START WITH THE GOOD?

Social media has the amazing power to bring people together and provide information in an unfiltered way. It allows people who, for whatever reason, cannot leave their home, or cannot communicate face to face to have a medium to bring the world to them in an effective way. It allows anyone to have a voice and an opinion and to be heard by a larger circle than those they could interact with or influence in a non-digital way. It gives a voice to the shut-in, the deaf, the physically remote people of a village up north, or those who are stuck in a hospital bed. It gives a voice to the shy, those who stutter, or those who have trouble articulating verbally. It allows for the transfer of unfettered information across international boundaries as well as the spread of ideas, in a quick and efficient manner. It has led to revolution and the toppling of authoritarian governments, and it has allowed for the quick and efficient activation of causes of all types.

Social media, when used to develop a personal brand, is a powerful ally. It allows us to demonstrate our worth, our ideas, and our values to a large audience of like-minded people. It allows us to engage in conversations that could not otherwise happen and build relationships across a country, a continent, or even farther. It allows us to share our ideas openly and learn from others, to discuss, have discourse, and learn things that we can internalize and integrate into our core values, if we so desire. It allows us access to opinions that are contrary to ours and a forum where those differences can be discussed in a non-threatening way. All of this helps in developing our own personal brand. By engaging with others in a meaningful and empathetic way, we learn more about ourselves, and we learn how to articulate what we believe is right and wrong. We can discuss ideas openly, listen, and learn.

All of this makes us more interesting to others because, if done right, and we listen to and respond to others more than we shout our own beliefs from the rooftops, relationships are built. It is through those relationships that trust is created, understanding of value is cemented, and others begin to discuss you and your ideas with others. Social media is not a one-way street. It is not about putting thoughts out into the "Twitter-sphere" and then ignoring them. It is the listening for the responses and engaging with those who engage with you that builds your brand. **No one cares about a talking head! People care about people who care about them and listen to their ideas and find value in what they say and do.**

26

THEN THERE IS THE BAD

Social media is a tricky thing. The way you perceive something, versus how others view and respond to the same thing, can be completely different. It is nearly impossible to convey real intention in 280 characters. Even emojis are not enough to ensure that everyone is on the same page and interpreting things as you do. That is the beauty of communication – it is based upon context. How you are feeling the moment you receive the information can affect your response. What happened to you that day or that week, how you feel about the person who sent you the information, and even how stressed, rushed, or distracted you are as you view something over social media can affect you as well.

It is not about the intent you had sending the information that matters as much as how it is perceived by those receiving it . . . and that is where things can get really interesting.

I am not sure how many people are familiar with the Dove campaigns over the last number of years. They have been mostly online, and focused upon the beauty of women in all shapes, colours, and sizes. For the most part, they have been extremely successful and well received. Well, things changed in October 2017 and if you Google *"Dove Soap Ads,"* you will probably be bombarded with a firestorm of controversy about an ad that ran for fewer than ten days and became a brand black eye for Unilever.

The ad was supposed to represent how all women are beautiful, and that colour of skin does not matter. Well, it did not turn out that way. In the ad, differently coloured women pull off their over shirt to reveal another woman underneath. The problem is that in this version of the ad, a black woman became white. Whether you agree with the controversy is irrelevant; people went crazy. Unilever ended up pulling this Dove ad and issuing a huge apology, because they were perceived as being racist.

To give you more details into this situation from many sides, I submit the blog post I wrote at the time titled "**Once Again, People . . . Perception is Reality.**"*

I am not here to debate whether this is right or wrong. **What I am here to say is that perception is reality.** My guess is that the vast majority of people who are screaming about this ad never saw more than this image. This is what they are basing as their view of Dove, and it is not good.

Google "Dove Commercials" and watch a dozen of them and decide for yourself what you think. My view is that Dove, for years, has spoken about beauty coming in all shapes, colours, and sizes, and that we are all special in our own way. To me, calling Dove racist seems incongruent with the body of work that they have done over the last few years.

What this teaches all of us is that we do not control the destiny of our own brands anymore. We can influence

---

* https://yourbrandmarketing.com/branding/
once-again-people-perception-is-reality

them, and we can tell the brand story, but it is how we are perceived by those who interact with the brand that really determines what our brand is.

Brands and companies, in general, need to realize that they will never make everyone happy. They need to determine who their audience truly is, understand why they care about the brand, and communicate with them in ways they can relate to, engage with, and champion.

I am sorry for all the bad press that Dove has received. In my opinion, they do not deserve it. Would there have been such a firestorm if a white woman tore off the sweater and became black? Maybe, maybe not! If not, what does that say about our society as a whole?

What does this have to do with your personal brand? It does not matter if it is a person or a company putting something out on social media; the effects can be exactly the same. In this case, and hopefully in yours, Dove has a strong enough brand and has built up enough equity in its brand that they can weather this storm. Depending on how people perceive you online, a misstep can be seen as just a misstep and can be forgiven. However, as you will see in the next section, lives can be ruined when people do not take the time to think before they engage online.

LAST BUT NOT LEAST, THERE IS THE UGLY

Justine Sacco, then the Corporate Communications Director for InterActiveCorp (IAC), boarded a plane from

London to South Africa on December 13, 2013, and her life changed forever. Justine was 30 years old and ruined her life with a 12-word tweet. At the time, she had only posted 407 tweets, was following 175 people, and had 1158 followers – a very small social media footprint at the time, but within a matter of hours, she was the number one trending item on Twitter around the world.

As she boarded the plane, she pulled out her phone, sent a simple tweet, shut off her phone, and settled in for a long overnight flight. The words that she tweeted were "Going to Africa. Hope I don't get AIDS. Just kidding. I'm white!" Justine could not have imagined what would happened next.

What happened next is that this tweet took on a life of its own. The haters started to hate, and the people who thrive on drama were enthralled.

While Justine slept, the Twittersphere stayed up talking about how horrific a person she must be. The firestorm was started, so the rumour goes, by an editor in Gawker's Valleywag, who sent it out to his 15,000 followers. It was then picked up as an article and the hashtag **#HasJustineLandedYet** went viral. By the time Justine landed in South Africa 11 hours later, millions of people had chimed in and retweeted the hashtag #HasJustine-LandedYet, and there were people waiting to take her picture at the airport when she landed.

One can wonder if Justine ever truly recovered from this. What we do know is that she lost her job and became infamous enough that her life was ruined for years.

I urge you to research Justine Sacco on your own and make your own decisions on whether she was misunderstood or not. The issue is that it does not matter whether she understood what she was doing; the damage was exactly the same. Once a picture, a comment, or a video makes its way into social media, it is there forever and has a life of its own. We, when crafting and shaping our personal brands, need to be ever cognizant of the Justine Sacco case, and many more like it. Lives can be ruined and reputations shattered in an instant because of poor brand management. I beg you to take a sober second look at any post you create or even share, before you hit the send key, to think about what the ramifications may be. You are just as culpable, in the mind of the crowd, for sharing questionable materials as the person who created them in the first place.

Understand that nowhere on social media, or anywhere that has a digital footprint, is completely secure. Facebook, Twitter, LinkedIn, Pinterest, Instagram, and all the other platforms are not 100% secure. People can find their way onto a page that you thought was locked down tight as a drum. The questionable photos that you have online that you think only your friends can see can end up on your friends' pages which are not as secure and then, privacy is gone. Think before you post. What you do today may be seen by someone trying to hire you five years from now, and that could cost you an opportunity, a job, marriage, or the embarrassment of someone who is close to you. We need to think before we post and realize that if we would not share information, thoughts, images, or whatever with the person in front of us, why would we do it from the "safety" of being behind a screen?

Develop and maintain a positive persona. Talk about things of value. Share things that are positive in the world, speak in thoughtful and not hurtful ways. It not only makes the world a better place, it helps secure your image, your brand, as one that is desired and respected.

ONE LAST THOUGHT ON SOCIAL MEDIA:

DO NOT be the person who just "likes," "hearts," "thumbs up," or whatever all the time. Tell people why you like their article; have an actual opinion. Tell people what it meant to you, what you thought about when you read it, and what else they may like if they enjoyed a certain idea. DO NOT be the person who connects with someone, and when they come back to you saying thank you for connecting, you ignore them. What is the point of connecting with anyone on social media if you are not going to engage? There is no prize for having the most followers. There is no prize for getting the most "likes," "loves," or "thumbs up." The prize is real human engagement and the building of relationships with people you might not have the opportunity to meet on the street. Either form a real relationship or don't. Either be authentic or don't. Either engage and communicate or don't. Whatever way you choose to use social media speaks volumes about you and your personal brand.

Now, I have focused a lot on social media. But, there are other forms of digital communication that will affect how others perceive your personal brand. Think about all the ways you communicate or how you do not communicate. Do you use technology to your advantage or do you hide behind it? How many people never return email? Do not answer voicemail? Do not respond to requests over Slack or an internal Wiki or whatever? Think about the people you are ignoring and how you are hurting your personal brand. By ignoring others, by not helping others, by not being generous, you are telling people a lot about yourself.

Do you want to be perceived as the unreliable person who cannot be counted on? How do you think that will play out next time you are up for a promotion or are a candidate for a job interview? Remember, all digital communication leaves a trace, and people look and communicate with others to find out about you. If you are not seen as reliable and trustworthy by others, based upon your digital signature, you are not! Now, what are you going to do about that?

CHAPTER SEVEN

ANTHONY C TAYLOR
MANAGING PARTNER AND LEAD FACILITATOR
SME STRATEGY

1. **What is your definition of a POWERFUL PERSONAL BRAND?**

You know the term: "your reputation precedes you," to me, that's a powerful personal brand. One that is recognizable, one that speaks to what your personal values are, what you bring to the table, and what people can expect from you.

Within that powerful personal brand, it should separate you from others, and in a way that has a polarizing effect on people: they either like you or they don't; as the brand you have to be content with that equation however it plays out.

2. **How has your POWERFUL PERSONAL BRAND allowed you to gain success in your industry?**

My industry, management consulting and professional services, has historically been dominated by large firms with high barriers to accessing their services primarily because of cost and perception. Because of my own personality, I've created a powerful personal brand around being approachable and friendly, which is contrary to typical stuffy "management consultants." As a thought leader, I provide my best content for free and in the process provide something that is extremely valuable. That has earned me, and my company, SME Strategy, a reputation of being high quality, high value, and approachable.

3. **What advice would you give to those looking to create their own POWERFUL PERSONAL BRAND?**

There are three things I would offer to anyone who is looking to create their own POWERFUL PERSONAL BRAND.

1) Stand for something. One of my favourite quotes is: "if you don't stand for something, you'll fall for anything." There's little power in being in the middle of the road on an issue. Yes, you'll agree with both sides, but in practice it provides uncertainty and confusion for the other parties.

Pick a side, take a stand, and let the chips fall where they may. That's power.

2) *Be authentic. Sophisticated people, people of experience, can sense when something is off. You may want to "fake it until you make it," but I've found that most of the time you're not fooling anyone when you're faking it, and it's pretty exhausting being "on" and disingenuous. Conversely, when you embrace your own self, and what you uniquely bring to the table, you bring an authenticity that is refreshing and ultimately communicates more effectively to the other party.*

3) *Take it easy. There's no one way to make a create a brand. That's the best part, you get to create what your brand is, you get to say how it goes. Everyone is making up their brand, and no one was born knowing what to do. So take it easy on yourself, and go with what feels right, and adapt as you go. Don't forget to have fun, even with something as "serious" as branding.*

4. **How do you perceive having a POWERFUL PERSONAL BRAND helps someone either secure a job or advance within a company?**

Why do people get hired in the first place? It's because a company or organization have a gap that they need filled. They hire the person that they believe has the characteristics to fill the gap and do the job. Short of doing the job for free and proving that you're capable, your brand, what you're known for, is what's going to let the person hiring know if you can do the job or not.

37

Think of how people Google things. You enter a query and Google presents you with things their extremely sophisticated algorithms suggest will be a good fit. Finding a job, or getting promoted are the same thing. The person hiring is looking for something, and you have the opportunity to create a personal brand that shows up as the number one on their search. If it's not the right match, they will move on to the next one.

CHAPTER EIGHT

NOW THE PROCESS BEGINS . . .

Now is the time to go back and reread the previous chapters with a new perspective. It is time to go back into your past and think about the things that have made you who you are today. Do not think that you will remember everything, or that everything in your past is vital to understanding your brand. People mostly remember the very good things that happen to them and the very bad. My hope for each one of you is that the list of good things far outweighs the things that were not so positive in your life. But, do not ignore the bad things. They happened! They are part of you, and the questions you need to ask yourself are "What did I learn from this?", "What has this experience taught me about myself?", and "How do I engage with others?" Every experience teaches us something.

Whether it is something that happened directly to you, or something that you watched happen to someone else, all experiences make you who you are and therefore, they all need to be learned from. The bad things teach us what we do not want to see in ourselves or others. This is a good thing! It gives us a baseline of what our moral compass is, which is an essential part of our personal brand. Take those negative experiences and tell yourself that these are the things that you do not want to emulate or traits that you want to demonstrate to others. Internalize it. Believe it. Do it! Your brand is as much, if not more, about the things that you disagree with as it is about the things that you agree with and embrace.

Look deep into your past, think about the things that have bothered you for years, and ask yourself why they still bother you. They shouldn't! Yes, they may have been painful and hurt at the time, but each of those experiences helped to determine who you are today. Celebrate that and let the past go. Take with you the learned experience from the negative action, but leave the hurt behind. Trust me, it is of little value, and you can never change what happened to you.

Be creative in how you look at the past. Write it as a chapter of a book or as a poem or a song that teaches you what you have learned from your past. This is not to share with others; this is for you. By codifying things, it makes them real. By articulating to yourself, and eventually to others, what you believe and why, based upon the experiences you have had, it makes you more comfortable in your own skin and frees you up to be a better you moving forward.

What are some of the lessons you can learn from your past?

CHAPTER NINE

LISA DAWSON
PRESIDENT
LJD MANAGEMENT

1. **How do you define a POWERFUL PERSONAL BRAND?**

I think the key word here is "powerful" since we all brand ourselves in one way or another (organically or strategically). So, the personal brand is simply how one markets oneself and profession such that you stand out from everyone else. Skills, personality and values are used to create your personal brand.

Now, a "powerful" personal brand might include strategy, measuring success of intended market penetration, and use of analytics so that your personal brand can be improved, adjusted for greater and greater success, and ultimately, a tool to help reach your business development goals.

2. **How has having a POWERFUL PERSONAL BRAND helped you gain success in yourb industry?**

   I am not sure I have a POWERFUL PERSONAL BRAND, but I can say that when I moved from just a business card, adding social media, learning from experts, never being satisfied with my current branding efforts, tracking, tweaking, and targeting one on one relationship building, my career improved.

3. **What advice would you give to those looking to create their own POWERFUL PERSONAL BRAND?**

   - **Self awareness** – *This is vital to finding and deciding on your niche/your brand/what sets you apart from the others in your professional space. Always be aware of yourself, strengths, weaknesses, how you are perceived, and where you can make a difference to those perceptions if you need to. Learn about your personality dimensions (innate behavioural preferences) and how that affects how you are perceived and how other types interact.*

   - **Brand everything you do** – *A brand does not begin and end with a business card and a website. It is in everything where communication exists!*

   - **Invest in yourself** – *Powerful branding does not happen between your ears. It takes courses, reading books, webinars, hiring a coach and many other resources to find out what works over time for you.*

44

4. How do you perceive having a POWERFUL PERSONAL BRAND helps someone either secure a job or advance within a company?

In order to secure a job, you have to stand out, be an attention grabber for the right reasons, and appear confident that you are the right person for the job. If you know how others perceive you or how your natural tendencies come across to others, then capitalizing on the positive and reaching deep to adopt behaviours to minimize the negative are branding techniques that might help you get that perfect job! As far as advancing in your current company, again, it comes down to knowing the business needs, who makes the decisions and how they perceive you. Adjusting your branding may include greater emphasis on values and abilities you have but are lesser known.

CHAPTER TEN

WHAT ARE THREE EXPERIENCES FROM YOUR YOUTH THAT MADE YOU *WHAT YOU* ARE TODAY . . . AND *WHY?*

When I was in grade six or seven, Chuck Taylor leather high-top sneakers were the "it" thing. Growing up where I did and going to the school I went to meant that I was exposed to a lot of kids who came from families far wealthier than mine. Not that I came from a poor background; I did not. We were middle class and lived in a reasonably sized house, but my parents never had any ambition to be the ones who "kept up with the Joneses." This came to a head the year all my friends got Chuck Taylor leather high-top sneakers, and I did not. I am sure that if my father thought it was the right thing to do, he could have paid for them, but he wouldn't. I am sure that I protested loudly and told my parents that they were being unfair to deny me such a necessity.

Looking back, and now with a child of my own, I get it. It was about teaching me the difference between a want and a need, what is important, and what is nice to have. We all have those in our lives – things we desperately want, but, do we need them? Is having that better car or bigger house going to make us a better person? Is it going to really affect our personal brand and how it is perceived by others, or are they just things? I am all for creature comforts, but they do not make me who I am as a person. You could take away my house and my car, and my brand would remain the same. Who I am as a person, and who you are as a person, should not be determined by the things in our lives. A million-dollar home is not your personal brand; it is a thing. It is an achievement that came from your success, but it is not you.

Take the time to think about the things in your life and whether they are a want or a need and how they influence your perception of yourself. For me, if you take away the love of my family, the respect that others have for me, and my desire to help others, then yes, you have taken away things of real value to me. If you take away my house or my car, I may be upset for a day or two, but I will go on, and thrive, as long as the core important factors in my life remain intact.

As the elder child in my house, I grew up being expected to sit at the table and converse with the friends of my parents. Looking back, this was one of the best things that my parents ever did for me. It taught me how to listen, how to converse, and about how to share controversial ideas in ways that people would accept, in premise, even if they were not ideas that they shared.

One of the people I met and learned to love and respect was a man who was a professional salesman. To the best of my knowledge, the man had no formal university education, but he was probably one of the smartest people I ever knew regarding understanding the human psyche. He grew up in the era of salesmen on the road and had all the stories to go with it. Many nights I listened to him tell stories about his adventures and the different products and services that he had sold over the years.

Then, one day, I had an opportunity to go and watch him live on stage. At this point of his career, he had become the pitchman for one of the educational seminar systems of the 1980s. This was the era where you filled a room with people who wanted to change their lives and showed them, for a fee of course, how you could teach them to do it. He never taught the course. Instead, he was the setup man, the guy (and in those days it was pretty much all guys) who came into town and convinced a room full of people that they had to sign up for that seminar TODAY. It was all about immediacy. It was all about demonstrating to people that their lives would change if only they would lay down their money TODAY, and take a course that would show them the path to riches.

Watching him in action was magical. The turn of phrase, the deliberate actions, and the timing were incredible. Day after day, pitch after pitch, the cadence was the same. The nuances that sold the program never changed from audience to audience, and the crowd kept buying. After a week or so, I had to ask him how he did it. How was the speech so perfect that it never seemed to change? It did not seem to matter if someone asked him a question in the middle of his talk. He would just answer it and move on like nothing ever happened.

This is where the magic of the persona came into play. Now, this was a man in his fifties, who looked about fifteen to twenty years older than he was. He had a slight hunch in his back, his beard and hair were grey, and he wore hearing aids. What I was about to find out from him was most of that was an illusion. The hearing aids were not hearing aids, but speakers in his ears. He had a tape recorder in his pocket, and it played his speech into his ear every single night. When someone asked a question, he put his hands in his pocket, thought a moment, said that was a good question, and answered it. What he was really doing was hitting the pause button on the tape recorder. When he was done answering the question, he would put his hands back in his pockets, pause and look at the audience for a moment, hit the play button, and start again. On top of that, the beard, the grey hair, the clothing, and the thicker glasses all were part of the act. It made people perceive him as being older and wiser and therefore more legitimate. What did I learn from this? Many things. Mostly, that a person will sometimes play a part to advance their objectives, but you need to look deep to see who people really are. My dad's friend was, and still is, one of the warmest, most generous, and dynamic people you will ever meet. However, when he was on stage, he was playing a part to gain an advantage. I leave it up to you to decide whether that is right or wrong. In today's world, those pitchmen and women still exist, but in far fewer numbers. That way of selling does not work as well or as often in an information society. It is too easy to be found out and too easy to be discredited.

The most important lesson that I learned was the magic that can happen when you are on stage. How, if you are prepared and honest in your craft, you can take an audience to places they have not been and teach them something of value. Words, and the turn of phrase, can be a powerful ally to help achieve goals and objectives. It is not as much about what you say, but how you say it, that can influence people in your direction.

In my teenage years, I rode and raced a road bike. It was a passion for me. Every week, I rode at least 400 km (250 miles) in training and raced pretty much every weekend from April to October. I wish I were as fit today as I was then. The best rides that I ever had were every Sunday with a group called the Cinelli gang. Cinelli is a high-end bicycle that is still in production. It had the best Italian components, was extremely lightweight, strong, and beautifully designed. I did not have a Cinelli; However, the owner of the bicycle store that I raced for and rode with every Sunday did. The owner of the shop rode in the British Empire Games and the 1948 Olympics. The people who were his friends were decorated riders from another era, and then, there were the young up-and-comers who rode with them, like me.

There are many things I learned from them, including how to ride safely in a tight pack of riders, how to attack coming out of a corner, how to figure out which riders will go hard and when, but those things are not what is important here. What is important is that they taught me dedication and the importance of working as a team. The dedication came from the fact that every Sunday, twelve months a year, whether it was sunny, raining, snowing, warm, or freezing, the Cinelli gang met at 8 a.m. and started to ride.

From my house to our meeting spot was a half-hour ride, and I picked up a friend along the way. Neither of us ever missed a week for years. It was more than dedication to a sport; it was a dedication to a family. I never wanted to be the person who let them down. To not show up meant the ride would have fewer riders, and the older ones would have to do more work going into the wind. I felt it was my responsibility, as did the others, to make sure that this ride continued to happen, and that the older riders got out and enjoyed it. Do not get me wrong; this was no meander. The owner of the shop was probably in his mid-sixties at the time, as were some of his friends, but they all could move. We just helped them keep the pace going up the hills, and they showed us the best ways to descend. Why is this story so important to me, and why does it make up part of my personal brand? The lessons I learned from these people about dedication, family, and teamwork was that the whole is much stronger than the individual parts. Those are characteristics that have grown up with me and have helped to make me who I am today.

⊟ What are the experiences you remember from your youth? What are the things that happened to you, either good or bad, that taught you valuable lessons about what you believe and who you are today?

_____

_____

_____

_____

_____

_____

_____

_____

CHAPTER ELEVEN

WHO ARE THE TOP THREE PEOPLE YOU ADMIRE . . . AND WHY?

This is a question that I pose time and time again, both in keynote addresses and in workshops. It really gets people thinking and produces some interesting responses. I want you to think about the people who have been direct influences in your life, or people that, through their actions, made you think or believe something differently.

This question is designed to make you understand more about WHY you admire people than WHO you admire. It is the WHY that makes all the difference.

Below are three examples from my life. These are people I had personal contact with and because of their actions and influence, they changed the way I thought about certain things. I will always be thankful to them for this. I have changed the names, but all other facts are consistent. I have not chosen family or close friends for the simple reason that I love these people and love is not a good enough reason, on its own, to emulate them. I admire them because of things I learned from them along the way, things I watched them do, and risks I saw them take no matter the odds stacked against them. They lived their lives on their terms, and their POWERFUL PERSONAL BRANDS acted as their moral compass.

The first person was my grade nine French teacher. What was so special about him? He was a linguist. French was not taught through nouns and verbs alone, but through the history and derivation of language. He took the time to explore with us where words came from, whether they were Ancient Greek, Roman, Saxon, or others, and how those words morphed through the years to come to their meaning today.

Why was this man such an inspiration? Because he was a teacher extraordinaire. He brought life to the classroom. He engaged his audience, day after day, class after class, and made things that would have seemed dull and boring alive and interesting. He took students who struggled with language and made it personal for them, so they could use their own curiosity and learn in ways meaningful to them. He demonstrated to me that education was about engagement and interaction and not memorization and regurgitation. He engaged us and allowed us to teach one another. He gave us the tools to not only be curious, but to articulate our curiosity and question when things did not make sense. In short, he inspired me to look for ways to get the most out of students and to realize that not everyone learns the same way. Being creative, in your teaching methods, helps you to teach more effectively. The added bonus is, that if you do this right, you get to learn from your students as well.

The second person whom I admire was also a teacher, but one who came to know me almost a decade later in the last year of my university life. I was in my final semester and decided that since I had room for a fun course, I would take a class in Finite Mathematics. I know: You are thinking what most of my friends were saying – I WAS CRAZY! But the reason I took the course was not because of the subject, but because of the professor.

I had met this Aussie socially during my years at the University of Victoria, and he was wild, wonderful, and full of life. He was middle-aged, recently divorced, and was enjoying his new found freedom. Saturday nights you could usually find him at the pub with either his guitar in hand or a pint in one hand and darts in the other. The darts were our mutual passion, and I got to know him playing round after round of 501. I had decided that if I ever had the time, I was going to take a course from him, just because I loved his passion for life. So, in my final semester, I did.

I remember sitting down in what was a first-year course as a fourth-year student. I sat up in the first or second row on that first day and he rolled in right on the hour. He put his name up on the board and said the following, almost word for word:

"Hello, this is Finite Mathematics 101, and it is a 100% final. You need two things to fail my course: you need to be stupid AND lazy. One of the two will not do it. You in the back, sit down, all the classes are 100% finals so you might as well learn from me. There will be three optional tests during the semester; they count for nothing, but if you do not take them, you are stupid! Here is my one rule . . . if one of you does not understand the lecture of the day, come up to my office afterwards and I am happy to help you; but if all of you do not understand it . . . it means I am a lousy teacher . . . and we will start again."

You could have heard a pin drop. One hundred kids were in the room and I am not sure what most of them were feeling, but I am sure some were terrified.

Sure enough, three weeks later, an hour into a lecture, he looked down at the front row. There were five or six of us who really got this stuff, and he knew it. However, that day all he was seeing was blank stares. So, he asked the question, "How many of you understand what I was just talking about?" When no one put up their hands, he rolled his eyes, muttered "stupid prof," erased the blackboards and started from square one.

What do I admire about him to this day? He was not afraid to be wrong. If he was wrong and if people just did not get what he was saying, he did not blame it on them. He took it on the chin, backed up, and started again.

The lesson here is that it is okay to admit when you are wrong or you do not know something. No one will ever blame you for saying, "I am not sure, so let me find out for you" or even, "I do not know." What people will not excuse is making things up or not owning up to your mistakes. Everyone makes mistakes, myself included. The people who are admired are those who can stand up and say "I made a mistake" or "I was wrong" and then work hard to make things right. That is the power of a personal brand. Being someone who people know will stand behind their word and do what they say they will do, every single time.

The third person I admire is a celebrity, but the name does not matter. I do not care that he is famous, instead I care that he speaks his mind, cares deeply about others and shares his view to make the world a better place for all.

What inspires me is his empathy, generosity, and creativity. This person is one of the most prolific writers I know and provides information that makes me think and makes me better at my craft. He speaks around the world, offers master classes, and shares ideas openly without hesitation. He believes that the world is better when we raise the level of the water for everyone. If we all get better at our craft, then the craft as a whole is better, and communication becomes more valuable because of it.

He believes that communication is built on listening, understanding, and trust. He looks to create a world where real conversation prevails, and where technology is a tool and not a crutch.

Because of him, I became a better marketer, a better listener, more empathetic, and possibly a better person. I was reminded over and over again that there can be hundreds of ways to look at any one problem and none of them are wrong. That point of view and context matter, and we are all the sums of our own experiences. Personal brands are built day by day by people who show up and do the hard work of introspection, critically looking at the difference between who they are and who they wish to be.

So, now I ask again: Who are the people you admire in your life and WHY? What are the experiences you have had that make you a better you? How are you incorporating this into your brand to make you more valuable?

Take some time, write things down . . . it is important!

_____

_____

_____

_____

_____

_____

_____

_____

_____

_____

_____

_____

_____

_____

_____

_____

_____

_____

_____

CHAPTER TWELVE

LUCIA FUENMAYOR
CHANNEL MANAGER
QUICK MOBILE

1. **What is your definition of a POWERFUL PERSONAL BRAND?**

It's your ability to showcase your skills in a way that transcends beyond your CV defined in both authentic online and offline presence.

2. **How has your POWERFUL PERSONAL BRAND allowed you to gain success in your industry?**

My personal brand has allowed me to gain success in my industry by allowing my superiors to feel at ease when investing in my growth as I have a proven track record of delivering results with tenacity.

3. **What advice would you give to those looking to create their own POWERFUL PERSONAL BRAND?**

Having a strong personal brand helps you secure your job by giving you the confidence and authenticity that make you an indispensable part of the workforce at your organization. Building your reputation and credibility make you an asset.

4. **How do you perceive having a POWERFUL PERSONAL BRAND helps someone either secure a job or advance within a company?**

Be aware of what you post on the internet. This is a powerful tool that can either help or hurt your career. When used properly, you can really elevate your personal brand by networking, sharing your thoughts and ideas and in turn, turning you into a source for knowledge in the topics you speak the most about. It is important to understand that your personal brand should not just revolve around your career, but it should also include some aspects outside of your work that make you unique, interesting and a lot more relatable!

CHAPTER THIRTEEN

WHAT ARE THE THREE MOST IMPORTANT THINGS IN YOUR LIFE . . . AND WHY?

We all have prized possessions. These are things that we either received as gifts or worked really hard for. The big questions are what are they, and why are they important to you? Each of you will have a different answer. You should cherish your memories.

It is not about the objects themselves, but the memories they elicit and the thoughts that fill your mind every time you look at them.

The first thing that comes to mind goes back over two decades ago when my wife and I first went to Alaska. My wife decided that she wanted a salmon serving plate. We entertain a lot and fish is something we both enjoy, so we figured that having a nice souvenir from the trip was important to us.

We have one rule when we travel. We purchase one thing and one thing only! We want a memory of the trip, but we want to be able to spend enough money on it to make sure that it lasts and is something that we both love.

So, off we went on a wonderful seven-day cruise to Alaska. Little did I realize how difficult a mission we had set for ourselves. Who would have thought that finding a salmon serving dish would be difficult in towns known for fishing? Let me tell you it was not an easy task. In every city, out we went through the stores in search of our salmon serving platter. Some platters were just ugly, some were just too small, but not one was just right. Seriously, I felt like Goldilocks looking for the salmon serving piece that was "just right"!

Well, believe it or not, we found it. It was in the last port, on the last day and late in the afternoon. It was ceramic, it had handles, it had a wonderful design in our kitchen colours, and it was perfect for us. So, we wrapped it carefully in bubble wrap, and then I carried it the rest of the afternoon in my backpack to make sure that it was safe.

When we got home two days later and I was upstairs unpacking, I heard this shriek of laughter from downstairs. I ran downstairs to make sure everything was okay, and there was my wife, laughing uncontrollably. When she finally stopped laughing, I figured out what she was saying. She told me to turn the plate over, and as I did, I started to laugh as well. The plate was made in British Columbia. We could have purchased it at home.

What did I learn from this? The journey is as important as anything else, and the story that comes out of the experience is priceless. Objects are objects, and without reference, they just become more things that clutter up the home. However, this serving dish had a story attached and a memory to go with it, and that is what made it precious.

The second thing that I held dear for years, until one day when it went missing during a move, was a worn, scratched, gold money clip. Someone else would have thought of this as something of little importance, but it broke my heart when it went missing.

WHY? Because it belonged to my great uncle. My dad's uncle was probably the closest thing I ever had to a grandfather. From an early age, I remember times spent together being fun. Even though he lived in Los Angeles and we lived in Vancouver, we saw each other often. I even have a memory of being ten or eleven and getting on a plane myself and flying down to LA to spend time with him. We went to Universal Studios and Disneyland, and I always remember him having a smile on his face.

The most famous quote I have from him was when I was a bit older, and he told me that he had bought a funeral plot because it was just him. He had bought one overlooking the hills of Santa Monica, and he said that the view I would have when I visited him would be wonderful, but his wouldn't. I laugh every time I think of that, and I think of the money clip he gave me, which he had for years. I miss both equally.

A third memory I have of an object is the car I am currently driving, a 2010 Ford Edge that I bought in 2012. Now, I am not a car person, never was, probably never will be. But this car is special to me for many reasons. Every car I bought before this one was old and cheap. I used them as long as they were safe and reliable, and then went out and bought something else. Always paid cash, never spent more than $5000. This car was different. It was the first car I bought off the lot, and I paid more for this one than I had for the last five cars I owned, combined. It was still used, but it was less than two years old. It had all the bells and whistles including leather, Bluetooth, and a moon roof. It was not the car that I was in love with; it was what the car represented to me.

It meant that the company I started in January 2008, in the middle of a recession, was finally doing well enough that I could buy the car I wanted, and I paid cash for it. It was a celebration of my success, and I could not have been prouder of myself. The first thing I did was take a bunch of pictures of the car and send out a LinkedIn post to all of my clients thanking them for their support over the years, and this car signified our success together. The car gave me a sense of accomplishment and a belief that good times were ahead. It reminds me to this day that relationships, hard work, and tenacity bring good things to your life, and that you should always be humble and appreciative of the things that come your way.

So, you may be asking, what does knowing what the most important things in your life have to do with your personal brand? You are the collection of your memories and experiences; embrace them. It is never about the objects; it is what they mean to you personally and the experiences you had gaining them. Think back to all the items you cannot bear to give away. We all have them. Each one is associated with a memory, and each of those memories is a learning opportunity for us about ourselves.

▣   What are your favourite objects, what makes them valuable to you, and what lessons have you learned by having them come into your life?

_____

_____

_____

_____

_____

_____

_____

_____

_____

_____

_____

CHAPTER FOURTEEN

WHAT ARE THREE IDEALS OR BELIEFS YOU HOLD ABOVE OTHERS . . . AND WHY?

Ideals and beliefs are personal. Understanding what we hold near and dear to us in terms of ideals and beliefs goes right to the core of our personal brands. They are also very hard for people to articulate. Beliefs can include "freedom," "family," or "integrity," but what do any of these words really mean? An only child with no parents or relatives can have a rich "family" life based on closeness they feel to friends. "Freedom" to someone in the jail means something completely different than to an entrepreneur and "integrity" to a politician may mean something completely different than it does to a priest. Each of us has to struggle with our own beliefs and find a way to articulate what we believe and why.

71

Many people will say that they believe in the freedom of the press, but when someone prints a full-page article in a newspaper, or posts an article online which speaks directly against what they believe to be true, they are not so quick to defend the freedom of the press. It is hard, because deep down we want people to believe what we believe. Guess what, that does not always happen, and the world is truly a better, more interesting place because of it. Knowing people with different viewpoints, ideals, and beliefs allows us to learn from each other. Part of having a personal brand is being confident enough in our own beliefs that we can have an exchange of ideals with others, listen to, internalize, and understand other people's point of view without having ours threatened. Embrace diversity; it makes your brand stronger.

Of all the beliefs that make up my personal brand, **diversity of thought** ranks near the top. I believe that there is no one true answer for anything and through discourse and exchange of ideas, we can always develop better, more evolved answers. This does not mean that I am beyond telling someone that they are wrong and digging in my heels; I am not perfect, but I believe in it and I strive towards this goal.

WHY? An exchange of ideas allows us to better understand one another's hopes, wants, needs, fears, and desires. They allow us to create things that are better because they happened as a result of the exchange of ideas, ideas that are greater than the sum of their parts.

Through listening and understanding, we can develop new concepts, new ways of approaching problems, and develop solutions that are significantly more effective in the long run.

The second ideal that I hold close to my heart plays off of the first one. *There is no such thing as a dumb idea, and anyone can develop a great solution.* This plays into my thoughts on leadership and respecting others. Anyone can come up with a brilliant idea, and that should be something to be celebrated by all. You do not need to be a Ph.D. or someone with twenty years of experience to realize there may be a different way of looking at something. Fresh faces produce fresh ideas, and realizing that can allow for innovation to occur in the most stagnant of places. Be the person who listens to others, who asks others for their opinions, and who fosters open communication. Personal brands built on "I know best and no other opinion other than mine matters" lead to ill opinions of that person moving forward. Those who can be comfortable in their own skin believe that when everyone works together, good things happen and credit is to be shared and draws people towards them. They are the leaders people want to follow, and it is their core beliefs, their brand, that makes that happen.

The third ideal that my compass points to is **honesty and integrity.** I know they are not the same thing, but they go together. I learned early on in my career that when you say what you do and do what you say, people will respect you. If you make a mistake, own up to it. If you do not know, do not make things up; say you will find out and get back to people . . . **AND DO IT!** Treat people fairly. You do not have to be the least expensive; actually, you never should be, but you need to be able to demonstrate and articulate that you are providing value. When you promise someone you will get back to them with information, make sure you do. If you said you would get back to them by 3 p.m. and it is 2:45 p.m. and you still do not have an answer, don't shirk your responsibility. Call them and let them know that you are still working on getting them information. Under-promise and over-deliver! Do not hide from problems. Face up to them and fix them; you will always be respected for that. Those who hide and blame others have a personal brand that you do not want or need.

▪ So, what are three ideals or beliefs you hold above others and why?

_____

_____

_____

_____

_____

CHAPTER FIFTEEN

SHAWN HALL
PRESIDENT
APOGEE PUBLIC RELATIONS

1. **What is your definition of a POWERFUL PERSONAL BRAND?**

A POWERFUL PERSONAL BRAND is distinctly yours – it is what sets you apart from the noise and brings you to mind when someone thinks about people working in your field. It requires that through actions you have imparted a clear understanding of the value, and the values, you bring to the table.

2. **How has your POWERFUL PERSONAL BRAND allowed you to gain success in your industry?**

By definition a POWERFUL PERSONAL BRAND is not generic or opaque, and will only be effective if your stated brand aligns with what people see in your actions.

A personal example – through feedback, I know I'm perceived as direct, one who will give clients and executives un-varnished perspective on a communications challenge and what is needed to address it. Some people don't like that approach, find it overly blunt, while others value the approach.

3. **What advice would you give to those looking to create their own POWERFUL PERSONAL BRAND?**

To have a POWERFUL PERSONAL BRAND requires putting forward the best version of your professional self, and not trying to be all things to all people.

CHAPTER SIXTEEN

WHAT WERE THREE WORK EXPERIENCES THAT HELPED SHAPE YOU . . . AND WHY?

Back in the late 1980s, I worked at a restaurant named The English Bay Café, that unfortunately no longer exists. It was in downtown Vancouver, and at the time it had one of the best reputations in the city. The food was delicious, the service was impeccable, and the view was incredible. The main dining room faced the water, and patrons were treated to incredible sunsets.

This was a time when people ate out and were loyal to various establishments. As a waiter, I had regular tables and guests who came in as many as three times per week. This was not a restaurant that hired just anyone. If you did not have waiting experience at another fine dining restaurant, there was no chance you would ever get a position in the main dining room. Perhaps you might have been hired for a position at the more casual main-floor restaurant, but to be invited upstairs to work was a real honour. This was also a time where service training was key. Everyone, no matter how many years you had worked elsewhere, started busing tables. You started during the lunch rush, worked up to busing tables at dinner, were mentored by a senior waiter on staff, and when the mentor decided, along with the general manager, that you were ready for your own section, you were given your white full-length apron.

I had two sets of patrons who I remember to this day, and they need to be mentioned here. The first was a husband and wife, and her sister, who came in two to three nights per week, fifty weeks per year. To this day, I have no idea what they did for a living, but cooking dinner did not seem high on their list. Those were the days when you were allowed to smoke in the restaurant, and both sisters smoked. At the beginning of each evening, a fifty-dollar bill was placed under the ashtray. If there ever were more than two butts in the ashtray tray, the fifty was removed and so was your tip for the evening. This game went on as long as I was at the restaurant, and I never remember having the fifty removed. What did this teach me? Listen to clients and pay attention to details. If your clients, friends, partner, or whoever are trying to tell you something, it is usually in your best interest to pay attention, listen, understand, and engage.

The other client that I remember vividly was a lumber merchant. He was a man in the 1980s who spent close to $10,000 per month in our restaurant and sometimes never showed up. He sent his clients to our restaurant daily, had them taken care of, and took care of the bill. When he did show up, there was a reserved table, literally with his name on it, and special china that no one, but he and his guests ever used. He had his own wine stored in our cellar and had a few things that were off the menu that were always made for him upon his request. Yes, he was rich, and yes, he was influential, but that is not the point of the story. The story centers on the fact that whenever he showed up, he called all the staff by name. He had the chef come out to talk to him personally, and he made sure that he tipped each person who helped him that day personally instead of just handing money over to the waiter and having him divvy it up. He took the time to care about the people around him and asked about wives, girlfriends, and kids. In short, he acted like a human being. No one was beneath him, and everyone deserved his attention.

Unfortunately, this is a trait that is becoming rare today. Think about it. What does it hurt you to take the time to be curious about the lives of the people around you? What benefit is there to being self-absorbed? Take the time to be passionate about people, and they will reciprocate.

The second work experience that taught me valuable skills was working for my father's commercial general construction company. My father was not the type of person who saved the plum jobs for me. I learned to dig ditches, sweep up job sites, drive halfway across the city in rush hour to pick up a vital part, and I was the hands-on apprentice for most of my dad's sub-trades. The deal was that I would be paid the same as everyone else on site, and I was expected to do the same work. I did not work for my dad; I worked for his foreman. From early on, I was told that if the foreman fired me, I was fired, and there would be no fighting it.

Now, the biggest thing I learned in the business was the phrase "whatever it takes." It was the mantra of my father and everyone who worked for him. He realized that the construction business was not about being the least expensive; it was about providing the best service and taking care of your clients. It was about understanding needs and challenges without having to have them explained. It was about doing the little things to make it easier for clients to do business with you and put their minds at rest knowing things would be done right and on time.

Let me elaborate. My father's company dealt in the commercial renovation business, and his largest client was with him for over 30 years. During that time, the client would go out every once in a while and bid a project, accept a lower bid, have someone else do the job, and then come running back to us. WHY? Because my father knew where the skeletons were in each building. He had renovated each store so many times he knew the history of what had gone on before, what problems they could run into, what little details needed to be focused upon, and what it would take to do the job right and on time. He was never the lowest quote, but when the store had to be open to serve people at Christmas, my dad's crews were off the floor, and the store and its customers were never affected.

His brand with that client was the person who would take care of them. The person who, if he promised something would deliver, and if he quoted a price and the scope of work did not change, he would honour it. He had a brand of thinking long term and being a relationship manager and partner for his clients. He could do this because his sub-trades always knew he would take care of them. What is the lesson from this? **Be a person of integrity!**

The third experience came early on in my marketing career. I had landed a large government agency which did a lot of printing. I built a relationship of trust with the key stakeholders, and they decided to trust me with a fairly large and important presentation document that was being delivered to their key stakeholders. This was in the days when we were moving from film and plate technology to direct to plate. In the old system, four pieces of film were made for every sheet, a composite proof was created and shown to the client, who then signed off on it. Then, the printing plates were made from those exact pieces of film. However, this was not a film and plate job; it was using the new direct to plate system. What this meant was that the file was output on a colour plotter, clients signed off on this, and then the file was resent to the plate maker to make the plates.

In this particular case, we made the proof, and there was a spelling error on the page. The client asked for another set of proofs, and we obliged. The client looked at the area where the spelling mistake was, signed off on the proofs, and off we went to press. However, what I did not realize, nor did the client, was that when we fixed the spelling mistake, we created a reflow of the document. This meant that somewhere on the page, the formatting got messed up and in the end, the entire document looked horrible because of it.

Well, I was young and naïve enough to think that if the client signed off on it, it was 100% their fault; technically yes, but in reality, not so much. I dug in my heels and insisted that if the client had signed off, the fault was theirs and they should bear the full cost of the reprint. The client said ok, we delivered the finished product, were paid, and the client never returned my phone call again.

I won the battle and lost the war. Yes, people need to be responsible for signing off on proofs, but in this particular case, with the new technology and the fact that I did not look to see if there were any other issues, I was just as culpable as he was. The right thing would have been to split the costs, salvage the relationship, and move forward. Anyone can make mistakes; it is how you deal with those mistakes and how you fix them that either builds or tears down your brand reputation. What did I learn from this? Think long term! Look at what is in the best interest of everyone involved and understand what a short-term loss can win you in the end. People will always respect someone who makes a mistake, owns up to it, and works to make it right. Those who run and hide when a mistake is made, quickly and permanently lose respect and brand credibility, which may never be recovered.

⊡   So, what were three work experiences that helped shape you . . . and why?

_____

_____

_____

_____

_____

_____

_____

_____

_____

_____

_____

_____

CHAPTER SEVENTEEN

WHAT ARE YOUR THREE FAVOURITE SONGS OR MOVIES ... AND WHY?

This was actually a section of the book I needed to really think about. There are so many songs and movies that have meant so much to me over the years, it was tough to narrow it down to three.

I will admit that I am an old soul. Many of you are going to look at these titles and ask, "How old is he?" The reason I picked these, besides the reasons outlined below, is because each one of them tells a distinct story. There is a moral built in and every time I watch the movies and listen to the song, I am reminded of lessons learned through their message.

Singin' in the Rain, with Gene Kelly, Debbie Reynolds, and Donald O'Connor is a classic. The music and dance routines are epic, and no matter how many times I watch it, it brings a smile to my face. WHY? Triumph over adversity. Beyond the happy little song-and-dance numbers is a story of the actors who are forced into changing their medium with the invention of the talking picture. The style of acting needed to change, dialogue needed to improve, and quite frankly, so did the acting. It was a monumental shift, and actors either thrived or vanished in the move towards talking pictures. Actors who were not capable of acting, directors who were not comfortable with the new technology, and voice sync that just did not sync properly were three of the challenges in the move to talking pictures. To cut to the chase, the first tests were a flop, but with some ingenuity and perseverance, in the end, they succeeded.

This is what I take from this movie: We all face challenges. We are all thrown into situations that are unfamiliar and uncomfortable at times; it is how we deal with them that enables certain people to flourish. If we can understand that new does not mean wrong, it just means different, we can all develop coping mechanisms that allow us to become better versions of ourselves.

It's a Wonderful Life, starring James Stewart and Donna Reid, is an American classic. Since 1946, it has played on big and small screens and has become a Christmas favourite. WHY? It teaches each of us that we matter. Every human being has value and contributes to the betterment of the world in some way. Some people make smaller contributions and some larger, but all are necessary, in concert, to make the world a better place. It is up to every person to understand their individual value and what they can contribute to make their part of the world a little better for all. Small acts have ripple effects and can cause chain reactions. Take the time to understand how what you do affects others. Realize that no one acts or lives in a vacuum. How you treat others will affect how they treat other people, and how generous you are with your time could affect whether someone else is given the time that they need from someone else. Be the change you wish to see in the world and create a personal brand that is a model for others to emulate.

In terms of a song that is close to my heart, *The Boxer*, by Simon and Garfunkel, is probably near the top of the list. Take the time and listen to the words:

In the clearing stands a boxer
And a fighter by his trade
And he carries the reminders
Of ev'ry glove that laid him down
Or cut him till he cried out
In his anger and his shame
"I am leaving; I am leaving."
But the fighter still remains, mmm mmm

To me, this song is about never giving up. No matter how hard life is, no matter what is stacked against you, you need to find a way to keep going. It is about perseverance and a belief that things will get better. It is a belief in yourself that you have the tools to move beyond adversity and step back into the light.

Think about it. How many times in our lives have we been thrown into something that we did not understand and had no idea how to fix, but somehow, some way, we got through it? The lesson from this is that no matter how tough things get, we all have the tools at our fingertips to make things better. This tool may require asking for help and being uncomfortable for a while, but no matter what, you need to believe that you can get through it. Belief in yourself and the belief that things will improve is a powerful dimension of a personal brand. Optimism is a powerful ally and allows us to find ways to solve problems that seem hopeless. If I can ask you to do one thing for me, teach this skill to as many people as you can. The world needs more people who believe that things will and can get better with time.

⊟   So, what are your three favourite songs or movies . . . and why?

_____

_____

_____

_____

_____

CHAPTER EIGHTEEN

GARRY PRIAM
PRESIDENT
MOSSA INTERNATIONAL

1. **What is your definition of a POWERFUL PERSONAL BRAND?**

   A POWERFUL PERSONAL BRAND is about creating a real and recognizable reputation for you and your company. It's part of your DNA and your company's culture. It radiates from you, exemplifies who you are, what you bring and the qualities that help define you as a person and organization. It's genuinely who you are.

2. **How has your POWERFUL PERSONAL BRAND allowed you to gain success in your industry?**

   Through my company, Mossa International, we help organizations and their people move towards success. This includes leadership and team development, coaching, enhancing communication and resolving conflict. We do this by really getting to know organizations at a granular level, by truly understanding the problems and the people involved and working with them and including them in finding a solution. When we look around us, we are all simple people with similar wants, needs and problems. I've always been a leader and many people see these qualities in me from when I played professional basketball to helping organizations win their own championships.

3. **What advice would you give to those looking to create their own POWERFUL PERSONAL BRAND?**

   In order to build a great reputation, become a good problem solver and be someone who people can feel comfortable coming to, you have to be willing to honestly listen to what is actually being said and not just what you think you are hearing.

4. **How do you perceive having a POWERFUL PERSONAL BRAND helps someone either secure a job or advance within a company?**

   Be yourself. Listen to who you are inside, be genuine and be willing to help others.

CHAPTER NINETEEN

WHAT ARE THREE EXPERIENCES FROM YOUR ADULT LIFE THAT YOU WILL NEVER FORGET ... AND WHY?

In the spring of 2000, I took an incredible trip to Portugal. Those were the days before cell phones and email coverage would have been expensive. I informed my clients that I would be away from the office for three weeks, told people in the office that I trusted them to handle things while I was gone and headed off.

During those three wonderful weeks, I did not check email once. We called home once or twice to talk to family, but that was it; the business was left far behind.

When I got back, there were a few issues, but nothing major. However, when I opened up my computer, there were over 3000 emails waiting for me. I know, by today's standards that seems a bit light, but then it seemed insurmountable. What did I do? **I DELETED THEM!** All 3000 emails were deleted without even looking at them, and a blind cc'd email went out to suppliers and clients alike that read "Hi, I just came back from three glorious weeks in Portugal. Unfortunately, when I got back, I had 3000 emails waiting for me. I have deleted them. If there is anything pressing that still needs my attention, please email or call me, and I will take care of it right away." So what was the response? There were five pressing emails for issues that needed to be handled, and fifty to seventy-five emails welcoming me back and wishing they had the guts to do what I did. Nothing got missed, clients were taken care of, and fifteen to twenty hours of my time were gained by not having to weed through each email and respond to it, only to find out it had been dealt with.

Why do I tell this story? It is about understanding what is important, what is vital, and what is a nice to have. It would have been nice to be able to respond to each customer, tell them I had a great trip, and I was now back and ready to take care of them, but this was not a great use of my time. It was vital to make sure nothing critical happened while I was gone that needed my immediate attention, and it was important to let everyone know that I was back and ready to take care of them.

It is about understanding that taking care of situations and being responsive are vital to corporate success, but it is also vital to make sure that you build in time for yourself. You cannot be at your best one hundred percent of the time. Taking vacations or just time away from the office is critical to recharge your batteries and put you back in the right frame of mind. It is important to make sure, however, that if you are going to be away, people are not left in the lurch. You need a process in place, so people know where to turn in your absence, and those who are taking care of things for you while you are gone are prepared for what may come their way. Part of your personal brand is about creating confidence in others that things will not fall apart if you cannot handle them personally. Being a control freak helps no one – not your fellow employees, not your boss, and certainly not your clients.

In 1990, my only grandparent that I had ever known, my dad's mother, died. I was living abroad in Israel at the time and had just come home a month earlier. It was impractical for me to go to the funeral. Now, let me preface this by saying, this is the only grandparent I ever knew. My two grandfathers both died when my parents were young, and my mother's mother died when I was about a year old. You might assume that I was extremely close to my grandmother, but I was not. We lived in Vancouver, she lived in Chicago, and quite frankly, that was the way my father liked it. She was a woman who died mentally long before her physical death. She was extremely negative and depressing, and had moved into an assisted care facility at about the same time most people were looking to retire.

To this day, I do not know what drove her to live a "glass is half empty" life, but the lesson I learned was that I want to live a life with "a refillable glass." Living a life of regret and remorse is no way to live. We all have things that have been difficult in our lives, and we all have experiences that we have not enjoyed that might even have been traumatic; however, we cannot let those experiences define who we will become. It is up to all of us to learn from those experiences, find out what was good, what was bad, and find out what we can do to make our lives better because of them. Take the time to think about the experiences and people in your life who have been negative influences. What have they done, or said, to create negative feelings within you? What can you learn from those experiences and how can you change your life so you are a better person because of it?

My experience, or lack thereof, with my grandmother allowed me to realize that I cannot afford to dwell on the negative, that I cannot afford to be bitter or hold a grudge. She taught me that life is full of wonderful experiences, and it is up to me to realize what they are and appreciate them. What have you learned from the negative experiences in your life, and what are you going to do to turn those into something positive?

The third experience that helped shape who I am happened on April 8, 2013, a day that I will never forget. It started with me heading to the local Safeway to pick up some chips for a barbeque that we were having that night and ended up altering my life forever. I was waiting to make a left hand turn into the parking lot, and without any warning whatsoever, I was rear-ended by two cars. The driver in the first car was not paying attention; the second driver was following the first too closely and was speeding. I broke no bones, had no blood gushing from my head, my airbags did not deploy, but from that moment on, I was deemed handicapped. I got a concussion, and quite frankly, it took months to properly diagnose. The concussion showed itself with spells of dizziness, mood swings, aphasia (knowing the right word, but not being able to verbalize it), the lack of ability to concentrate over long periods of time, and numerous other symptoms.

The resulting lawsuit took four years to wind its way through the judicial system. I saw more experts than I could count, my business almost went under, I was in rehab during the entire process, I wrote a six hundred and fifty-page journal about what happened to me on a daily basis over the four years, and my family suffered because of my personal frustrations. During the entire process, my family and friends could not understand what the problem was because it was nothing that they could physically see. With a brain injury, there is no physical evidence, and therefore, demands were made of my time that I just could not honour, causing frustration between me and my parents. Loud, crowded rooms became impossible for me, because of something called hyperacusis (inability to regulate noise volume) and tinnitus (constant ringing in the ears), and therefore we did not see very many people socially for almost four years.

At the end of the fight with the insurance company, in early February 2017, all that I received for all of my grief was a cheque, and certainly not a number that would change anyone's life.

Why do I share this with you? Because you cannot be defined by the trauma of your past. I have built a series of work-arounds that have allowed me to make my life as good as I can be based upon my circumstances. We have our favourite restaurants that we can go to, where we know we can sit in a quiet corner, and I wear hearing aids that act as noise reduction headphones. I write things down now because I do not remember things long term as well as I used to, and when I teach, I give my clients more frequent breaks because it is not only better for me, it is better for them as well.

In short, I have created processes that allow me to be as close to my old self as I can, realizing that I have limitations. It does not affect my quality of work, it does not affect those who I work for or work with, and it allows me to continue to be productive and useful.

HERE IS SOMETHING THAT I LIVE BY:

The glass is not half full, nor is it half empty; it is refillable!

What is my lesson from this? We all have adversity in our lives. Hopefully, most of you have experienced nothing so traumatic, and those who can top me, I am sorry. However, no matter who you are, no matter what your challenges are, it is up to you to decide whether those challenges are going to define you in a positive or negative way. We can all retreat to the couch, turn on the TV, and stay there the rest of our lives, but what good is that going to do you and those around you? It is up to you to realize what you can do to make the most of the situation you are in. It is up to you to develop processes and procedures that allow you to make the most of your life. No one is saying that it is easy, but I promise, by taking the time and making an effort, it will help you develop your POWERFUL PERSONAL BRAND.

▣ So, what are three experiences from your adult life that you will never forget . . . and why?

_____

_____

_____

_____

CHAPTER TWENTY

SO, WHAT HAPPENS WHEN THINGS GO WRONG?

As Forrest Gump's momma told him, "Life is like a box of chocolates, you never know what you're gonna get."

Life is unpredictable, and sometimes, it seems to hit you with way more than you bargained for. Floods, fire, death, abuse, and many other horrific things happen to people every day. There does not seem to be a reason why at the time, but there are times in our life when we are faced with challenges that make us question whether good truly does exist.

But what do you do? Do you sit there and wallow in the misery? Do you give up, throw up your hands, and wait to die? Do you blame everything and everyone and become bitter and resentful?

Unfortunately, some people do . . but you should not! Take it from someone who has been in some horrible situations that eventually, things do get better. Life does move on, and with the perspective of time, we can heal. It takes time, effort, and a lot of soul-searching, but it is possible. The trick is to believe the world can get better.

There is a story of two identical twins, one an optimist and one a pessimist. The story is most famously attributed to Ronald Reagan, but its true origin is unknown to me. They take the pessimist child and put him in a room full of the best toys and then take the optimist and leave him in a room full of horse poop for an hour. When they come back, the pessimist is sitting in the centre of a room full of broken toys and crying. They pick him up, console him, and send him on his way. Next, they go into the room with the optimist. There is horse poop everywhere, and the kid is covered in it. They finally get a hold of the kid and stop him from flinging the poop and ask him what he is doing. The optimist answers "with all this horse poop, there has to be a pony in here somewhere."

Be the optimist! Realize that every situation, no matter how bad, can teach us something about ourselves and the world around us. Take the time to figure out how bad things affected you and learn how you can become stronger because of them. Remember, adversity is everywhere; it is how we deal with it that determines whether we have a POWERFUL PERSONAL BRAND or not.

CHAPTER TWENTY-ONE

WHAT ARE YOU PASSIONATE ABOUT ... AND WHY?

Being passionate is a critical piece of developing a POWER-FUL PERSONAL BRAND. We all have things that we like, love, hate, admire, abhor, idolize, and/or demonize. It is our ability to care about, or rail against things, that make us uniquely human. Too many people live their lives playing it safe, not willing to commit to anything, not even love. They are so afraid of being seen as not part of the "norm" that they live their entire lives in a noncommittal state. We have all seen these people, and some of us are even related to them. These are the people who are so afraid of what others may think of them that they will never say or do anything that could be seen as having an opinion one way or the other.

To me, this is the worst kind of existence. It is a death sentence early in life. To not have emotional ties to anything or anyone, due to fear of what may happen, cuts you off from all that is great about life. **Life is unpredictable, and it is that unpredictability that makes life wonderful.** It is that unpredictability that makes life wonderful. It is the risks that we take, with the possibility of rewards, which makes taking risks worthwhile. No one is guaranteeing you things will be easy, nor are they guaranteeing you that things will always turn out the way you want, but so what? Whether you win or lose, you learn from the experience, and your life is far richer because of it.

I am passionate about life and taking calculated risks. Owning my own company is a risk each day. Standing up on stage and speaking in front of hundreds or thousands of people is a risk every time that I do it. Writing this book is a risk. You may like it, you may hate it, but if I did not write it, I would never know. Taking risks and being passionate about what you believe allows you to do things you would not necessarily do. Why am I passionate about these things? Because they make me feel alive! Taking risks and doing what I believe is right, no matter what the odds are, allows me to believe that I am who I believe I am. I do what I think needs to be done, and I build a stronger belief in myself through the process. By my having this sense of confidence, others see it and want to be around me and understand more about what I believe in.

Think back to the first time you tried something new. It was scary. It was the fear of the unknown. It was the fear of failure, or worse, of people seeing you as a failure, and laughing and talking about you. Scary, wasn't it? But what happened? More than likely, everything went well, and you accomplished your goal. You were proud of your achievement, and others around you recognized you for your actions taken.

Being passionate is all about risk and reward. Being passionate enough to speak up and speak out either for what you believe to be true or against what you vehemently oppose. Taking a stand, no matter how big or small, says something about you and your POWERFUL PERSONAL BRAND. It says this person is interesting and should be paid attention to because they are willing to stand up and articulate and act based on their beliefs.

"You have to understand your own personal DNA. Don't do things because I do them or Steve Jobs or Mark Cuban tried it. You need to know your personal brand and stay true to it."

– Gary Vaynerchuk

So, what are you passionate about? What do you believe in? What would you fight for and what would you fight against? What would you do even if you knew the entire world was watching and would judge you positively or judge you negatively?

CHAPTER TWENTY-TWO

PHILL DOMASK
PRESIDENT
THE PHILL DOMASK CONSULTANCY

1. **What is your definition of a POWERFUL PERSONAL BRAND?**

    A personal brand lives or dies based upon ongoing market-place and community opinions regarding who you are and what you bring to the table. For me, a POWERFUL PERSONAL BRAND proves meaningful to both the person and the marketplace and connects marketplace stakeholders to the person emotionally.

2. **How has your POWERFUL PERSONAL BRAND allowed you to gain success in your industry?**

    At the height of the 1981-82 U.S. recession, I graduated from college, passed the Wisconsin broker's license exam, and entered the real estate business. Too naïve to realize housing demand declines significantly when interest rates exceed 17%, I enjoyed immediate, though not spectacular, success. But blessed with youthful enthusiasm, a strong memory, affinities for numbers and financing, and passions for vintage architecture and local history, over time I became identified by other agents, appraisers, lenders, and property owners as the go-to guy for residential property information in Milwaukee's historic Bay View neighborhood. This identification opened many doors for self-promotion, as I became a trusted industry resource for local media and was offered opportunities to speak at career and homebuyer seminars, church and community group events and at association meetings for lenders and appraisers.

Starting in real estate circles and expanding to the community-at-large, people began calling me the Mayor of Bay View. Homeowners and homebuyers began to connect with me emotionally (if you were looking to sell or buy a home in Bay View, you would likely welcome the chance to talk with the "Mayor"). Because people found value in my demonstrated expertise, my business grew.

I have tried hard throughout my career to earn "go-to guy" identification in the marketplace. Today, being someone construction industry professionals readily turn to for advice on business growth (and rely on for effective planning, marketing, and business communication support) contributes greatly to successes – their success, and mine.

3. **What advice would you give to those looking to create their own POWERFUL PERSONAL BRAND?**

Realize upfront although you can and should develop and articulate your personal brand, marketplace assessment trumps brand aspirations and determines your personal brand reality. It would have been hubris to call myself the Mayor of Bay View. I remain grateful to whoever coined the nickname and to everyone who used it on my behalf.

Start your personal brand development with authentic self-assessment. Document (in writing) what you bring to the table – your clear strengths, specific areas of expertise, and reasons why you are a go-to person). Identify your core values – the basic elements of how you go about your work and what you are willing to fight for. Outline ways across your career you have delivered remarkable value. Catalog things you care deeply about. List ways you have made dramatic differences: at home, at work, and within the communities you engage.

Next, review your self-assessment efforts and circle those things your marketplace also cares deeply about. What is meaningful to both you and the market(s) you serve? What passions do you and the marketplace share (passions for vintage architecture, local history, and helping people realize their dreams fueled my real estate success)?

Recognize the problems your market shareholders face and develop and/or share tools to help shareholders solve them. Give market stakeholders a taste of your "go-to" proficiency by demonstrating your strengths, expertise, and values, online and offline.

Invest in some of the communication tools and tactics below to keep your marketplace engaged, demonstrate your proficiency, and help marketplace members succeed: (1) Produce a monthly newsletter with relevant information focused on marketplace success; (2) Send market stakeholders articles, eBooks, and other information supporting their success; (3) Be active on LinkedIn and other social media platforms; (4) Create a blog and/or regularly post articles relevant to stakeholder success on LinkedIn's In Publishing; (5) Produce a series of podcasts or YouTube and Facebook videos to share relevant information to help market stakeholders succeed; (6) Join and answer questions on Reddit and Quora; (7) Actively participate in associations serving marketplace shareholders; and (8) Speak at conferences, conventions, and Chambers of Commerce meetings.

Finally, set the stage for emotional connection in your marketplace by radiating spirit, energy, passion, and vitality in every task you undertake, every day.

CHAPTER TWENTY-THREE

HOW DO YOU VOLUNTEER . . . AND WHY DO YOU DO IT?

How we volunteer our time says a lot about us as people. I believe that the world would be a much better place if everyone volunteered somewhere doing something. It does not matter where, or how much; it is the act of volunteering that matters. WHY? It is the thought that there are people other than you in the world, and that we as a global community are stronger when we band together. It is the thought that everyone needs a hand up, not a handout, and if we can use whatever skills we have to make someone else's life just that little bit easier, they will become another contributing member of the global society.

Those who volunteer do so out of a sense of purpose, a sense that the world gets better when you get involved, that everyone has a role to play, and it is their role to help make their corner of the world a little better. I tend to volunteer in areas of educating youth. Being a mentor and an educator gives me great satisfaction because I help others improve and learn things easily that would otherwise be hard and frustrating. I lecture at the local universities and mentor their marketing and entrepreneur students as the needs arise. They are the future and have much to offer. The passion they have and the achievements they go on to do, once they leave academia, are awesome. I have followed the careers of some of the people I have mentored, and I have watched them take leadership positions within companies. I have watched them grow as individuals and become active in causes they believe in. That to me is the greatest success of my mentoring: to see others thrive and grow and eventually give back.

The act of giving back is the philosophy of paying it forward, giving time or effort to people who may never be able to repay you for your kindness and actions. It is about realizing you have skills others do not, and by donating time, expertise, or both, you can make someone else's life better and enrich your own at the same time. I am not negating philanthropy or charity, and yes, they are different. However, most philanthropists do not simply give money; they also invest time into the causes they believe in.

What are the skills you possess? What are you passionate about? How can you help others gain a foothold and improve their lives? None of this is charity; it is an investment in all of our futures. Charity is about feeding or clothing a cold and hungry person today; philanthropy is about helping develop systems and processes, so that people are not forced to be cold and hungry tomorrow. How can you invest your time and effort to help make people's lives better and in turn, build your personal brand by cementing the ideals you hold dear?

Looking for some ideas?
Check out www.givingwell.ca.

◧   So, how do you volunteer and why do you do it?

CHAPTER TWENTY-FOUR

THE POWER OF A PERSONAL MANIFESTO

Your manifesto is the codification of your personal brand. It is who you are, what you believe in, and what gives you the moral compass to do what you do on a daily basis.

Let me tell you the story about how having a POWERFUL PERSONAL BRAND, a manifesto, got a Canadian icon through a crisis that should have bankrupted and ruined his company.

I suggest looking this crisis up on Wikipedia because of the concise nature of the reporting, but all major news outlets do concur with this report.

It is not the Listeriosis crisis that is of particular interest to this book, but how Maple Leaf Foods, and the CEO, Michael McCain, whose family has owned Maple Leaf Foods for over 50 years, dealt with the crisis.

It is a case study in ownership of a crisis. The face for the crisis, during the entire time, was Michael McCain.

He did not push this crisis off to a public relations company, his legal or media team; he, himself, owned the crisis. He stood in front of the cameras, the shareholders, the stakeholders, and the employees and stated what happened, what was happening, and what was going to continue to happen until this crisis was remedied. Even once the crisis was over, Michael McCain took charge to make sure policies and procedures were put in place so that this would never happen again. He did not shirk responsibility, he did not try to lay blame elsewhere, and he did not try to make the problem disappear by ignoring it. That was the set of ideals that helped the company weather the storm. By seeing a leader with a POWERFUL PERSONAL BRAND at the helm handling the crisis, people felt confident there was true remorse, responsibility was being taken, action was underway, and no one was trying to sweep this under the rug.

How many times have we seen people try to run and hide during a crisis and only appear to attempt a mea culpa once the media has turned their full attention to the situation? What does that do to brands, either personal or corporate? Simply put, it can devastate them! Everything is easy, and people are happy when things are going well; it is how we handle ourselves in a crisis that truly matters. People are looking for someone to live up to their expectations of what is right and what is wrong and to lead through the crisis. If you can be that person, no matter how difficult it will be during the crisis itself, your brand and your reputation will be stronger in the long run.

Take time to really understand who you are, what you do, and why you do it. This manifesto, when codified, provides you with an anchor in the storm. Michael McCain has one, as do most great leaders. It is what helps them decide what to do when a crisis occurs. It gives them an understanding of who they are and what they should do.

BELOW IS MY PERSONAL MANIFESTO:

It can be summed up in these three simple thoughts.

- Make the world a better place when I leave than when I entered

- Do no harm to others

- Believe in possibility for myself and others and that good wins in the end

How did I come up with these three? By understanding the things that are important to me. NOTE: I have gone wide and deep here. This has taken me years to figure out, and I am not expecting anyone to come up with a list this detailed. I provide it to provide context for the manifesto above.

- I am a husband, a father, and a member of my community.

- I believe in the ideals of many over the ideals of one.

- I believe that there is no shame in the answer "I am not sure, let me find out for you."

- I believe that knowledge is to be shared and people are to be helped.

- I believe that the world is a better place with trust and honesty.

- I believe that friends and family are words not to be taken lightly.

- I believe that creativity and diverse opinions solve issues best.

- I believe that the best work is done through collaboration.

- I believe in putting in the effort to do a job properly the first time.

- I believe in working with your clients to achieve their goals.

- I believe that listening and understanding before doing creates a better solution.

- I believe that nothing worthwhile ever comes from doing things the quick and easy way.

- I believe that you get what you pay for.

▣ I believe that mentoring the next generation builds a better tomorrow.

▣ I believe that a great idea can come from anywhere.

▣ I believe that leadership is a privilege, and not a right, and comes with obligations.

▣ I believe in the future, and our past helps design it.

▣ I believe that people are responsible for their own thoughts and actions and must understand there are consequences for both, which apply to them.

▣ I believe that time and perspective allow for better decisions.

▣ I do not believe in absolutes or that there is always one right answer.

▣ I believe that there is a difference between listening to and understanding someone.

 What is your manifesto, and why do you believe what you do? This is important!

CHAPTER TWENTY-FIVE

MARK FIDELMAN
PRESIDENT
FANATICS MEDIA

1. **What is your definition of a POWERFUL PERSONAL BRAND?**

   A POWERFUL PERSONAL BRAND introduces you to an audience prior to meeting them. Ideally, it gives new, positive meaning to "your reputation precedes you."

2. **How has your POWERFUL PERSONAL BRAND allowed you to gain success in your industry?**

   Three major things: First, people seek me out based on my reputation. Second, networking doors are easier to open. Third, you are automatically given more authority in business situations which allows you to push for your ideas to happen.

3. **What advice would you give to those looking to create their own POWERFUL PERSONAL BRAND?**

   Write down your goals. Does a personal brand help or hinder those goals? Do you understand how much work and dedication it takes? A personal brand may not be for you, but if it is – throw everything you have into creating one.

4. **How do you perceive having a POWERFUL PERSONAL BRAND helps someone either secure a job or advance within a company?**

   This is tricky. I am more inclined to say that it holds people back in these situations because the hiring manager is fearful or intimidated.

CHAPTER TWENTY-SIX

YOU CANNOT FAKE AUTHENTICITY

Has "more authentic" joined "disruptive" as another nonsensical word in our vernacular?

I was in a discussion online with someone who said that they wished to "Be Crazy Authentic." To me, this seems absurd. Either you are authentic, or you are not. Either people see you for what you are, individually or as a brand, or they do not. Either you show people your warts and hope they are going to appreciate you anyway, or you do not. You are who you are – good, bad, and ugly – and by displaying this to the world, you are authentic.

No one can make everyone happy. I know this book will motivate some and not others, but that is okay. I say what I say because I believe it, and people will either embrace me for who I am and what I believe, or they won't. Those who do embrace me are part of my tribe. They see my value to them and relate to me and my brand for what it is. My brand is not for everyone, and again, that is just fine. I want to deal with people who value what I value and believe what I believe. I cannot change the world, nor do I expect to. What I can do is influence my corner, by being authentically me, saying what I believe to be true and act accordingly.

Take the time to understand who you are and what you believe. Authentic is not just a word without any real meaning or consequence; it is the heart and soul of who you are. When people see you as authentic, things happen. You may be seen as trustworthy, influential, or a leader. You may be someone who always speaks the truth or someone who does what they say. You may be funny, or you may be serious. You may be a combination of all of these, or none of these things at all. What I can guarantee, though, is that if you do not say what you believe and act accordingly, people will see through your inauthenticity and give you little thought.

⊡ What do you truly believe, and what is the authentic you?

_____

_____

_____

_____

_____

CHAPTER TWENTY-SEVEN

CREATING A CONCISE PERSONAL VISION STATEMENT

One last thing that you need to be considering when developing a POWERFUL PERSONAL BRAND is communicating your why. It is not enough to understand what you do and why you do it. You need to communicate your value in a way that is concise and engaging, and that allows people to quickly understand why they should be paying attention.

Think of it like the proverbial tree that falls in the forest. If no one hears the thud, did it truly fall?

Our brands are never developed, nor do they exist, without context. They only exist if someone, or a group, believes in them. We are only as valuable as how we are perceived by others, and effective communication of your value is critical in order for others to understand it.

To effectively demonstrate your value in a concise manner, you really need to have a personal vision statement. A personal vision statement is a short, concise statement about who you are and what you do.

Here is mine:

"I help brands tell engaging stories that compel their customers to take action."

In fifteen words or less, it is developing a statement that tells people what you do and why they should care.

Sounds easy?

It isn't!

I can tell you that over the last twenty years I have probably used more than twenty different personal vision statements, and each one has been usurped by another when I was able to craft something I felt better demonstrated the why others would find me of value. Some changes were small and others were complete. Consider the creation of a personal vision statement a quest for the ultimate elevator pitch. You have it in you, but it may take time and effort to get it right.

How do you get there?

Think of this as a three-step process:

1. You need to find out what you really like to do.
2. You need to find out what you are really good at.
3. You need to find ways that these two things help solve issues for people you wish to influence.

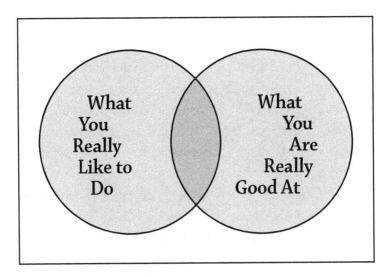

FOR EXAMPLE:

I like solving problems for people. Always have, always will. I love putting all the pieces together, understanding how they fit, and creating solutions that are reasonable and attainable based upon the situation placed in front of me.

What am I good at? I am good at developing and telling the stories of business-to-business companies that are mid-sized ($10-$100 million) in ways that compel their audiences to understand their value and want to engage.

My ideal customer is challenged with growth. They wish to capture greater market share and compete on larger projects, but they are having issues growing and do not know why.

Putting these three things together allows me to maximize my value as a strategic consultant for my clients. I can help them look at their business holistically; understand their goals, challenges, fears, desires, and opportunities; help them marry this understanding with the needs of their clients; and develop communication strategies that are based upon realities today and potential for the future.

Where does what you like to do, what you are good at, and the problem you can solve that others have collide? Notice, I did not say you had to be great at it; I said you had to be good. The intersection needs to include things you are better at than most. It is understanding how you can narrow the focus so that your talents and passions align with the needs of your clients. This may be the most challenging exercise in the entire book, but one that is critical to allow you to create a space that is yours. It is about developing a unique way to communicate your value to people who will value your work and can justify paying your wage. The best part of having a POWERFUL PERSONAL BRAND is that if others perceive your uniqueness and understand your value, price becomes less and less of an issue. It is up to you to be a problem solver and someone who helps others reduce stress in their lives. That is what success will look like in your future.

 Take the time here to figure out the intersection between what you love to do, what you are good at, and what those you wish to influence will find valuable.

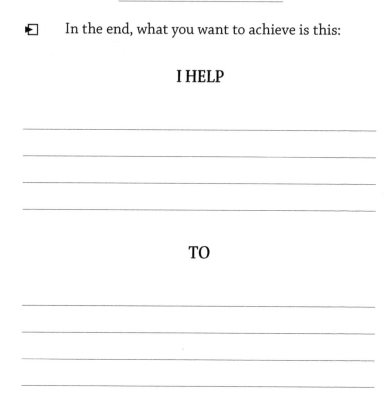 In the end, what you want to achieve is this:

I HELP

_____

_____

_____

_____

TO

_____

_____

_____

_____

CHAPTER TWENTY-EIGHT

PATRICK KELAHAN
FORENSIC MARKET STRATEGIST
H2M ARCHITECTS AND ENGINEERS

1. **What is your definition of a POWERFUL PERSONAL BRAND?**

The existence of an external perspective of the brand holder that matches closely with what the brand holder intended. This includes a balance of personal, public, and business relationships that are in balance for the three arenas.

2. **How has your POWERFUL PERSONAL BRAND allowed you to gain success in your industry?**

Instilled self-confidence through a continuous effort/reinforcement loop through all positions I have held, allowed me to leverage business skills into volunteering efforts, focused me on ensuring work/life balance is maintained.

3. **What advice would you give to those looking to create their own POWERFUL PERSONAL BRAND?**

Observe what others do – successful, struggling, eccentric, respected- all types of persons can provide perspective on how you forge your brand. It's not just where you want to be in business – it's how you balance demands on your time and efforts.

CHAPTER TWENTY-NINE

PERSONALITY TESTS YOU MAY WANT TO CONSIDER

There are literally hundreds of personality tests in the market today. Some are free and some cost hundreds or thousands of dollars and require experts in their field to administer and interpret. My hint to you is to get your hands on a few of them and look for consistencies. No two tests will give you the same results; they are based upon interpretation of data and algorithms designed by different people. Are any of them perfect? I say no, but I think if you can take a few of them and look at them in concert, you will have a better idea of who you are, what you like, and what you dislike.

In my opinion, taking personality tests, in aggregate, gives you more insight into your personality. They help you codify what you are good at, what you are not good at, what you like to do, and what you love to do. I believe that, in aggregate, they allow you to have a deeper understanding of yourself and help put you onto a path of success and happiness. Too many people are frustrated because they are in jobs and professions doing things they intrinsically do not like to do. By taking a series of tests, you can have a better idea of how you can be more successful in your career and understand where the pitfalls may be so you can avoid them.

Three sets of tests I have taken and think are of interest are:

1. www.16personalities.com

2. StrengthsFinder 2.0 by Tom Rath

3. Myers-Briggs

- **www.16personalities.com** is a freemium model. The basic test is literally 16 questions, done online, and I do not think the entire process takes more than 10 minutes. You will get a basic personality assessment immediately, and for free, but if you are looking for a more detailed analysis with more feedback, they charge you. Invest the few dollars if you are so inclined; you might find the extra insights interesting, as I did.

- **StrengthsFinder 2.0** by Rath is now owned by Gallup and is an interesting premise. The test is based on 36 personality traits, and the philosophy is that you should concentrate on your top five and find other people, with other strengths, to do the tasks that you are not good at. The idea is that you should not focus on your weaknesses, but double-down on your strengths. Why do your own accounting if you are not good at it and hate it? Better to hire an accountant. You should spend your time doing more of what you are good at and that will provide you with the funds to hire the people to do the other things and you will be further ahead.

The book is an interesting read; however, head to the back of the book first, if you are into hacks. At the back of the book there is an URL and a code for you to take the test. The feedback is immediate, in pdf format, and fairly complete, but it only focuses on your top five traits. If you are serious about this and really want to understand the entire range of personality traits, there are consultants who can walk you through a more extensive battery of tests, which will give you an even better understanding of what you do well and what you do not.

The third test is **Myers-Briggs**, a test that you need to take through an HR consultant. It breaks the world into 16 different personalities based upon how you answer a litany of questions. It is extensive, it is reliable, and it is accepted by the majority of people who administer tests as one of the gold-standard tests. If you are in a leadership position, I highly recommend having your company put you through this testing, or something similar. It will provide you with insights that will help you understand not only your personal brand, but those of others around you. Being able to understand others' brands and their strengths and weaknesses will make you a better leader of people and allow you to build a more POWERFUL PERSONAL BRAND for yourself.

CHAPTER THIRTY

SO, WHO ARE YOU?

So now I ask, who are you? Now that you have taken the time to read through all of this information and think about your life to date, and all the experiences, both positive and negative, who are you? Are you any closer to answering this question?

I think you are, but you may have to go back, reread certain chapters, and answer the questions I have put in front of you. Take the time to put down your thoughts in writing. This is why I gave you room at the end of each chapter to write. By actually taking the time to write things down, you are cementing ideas in your brain and working out reasons why you do what you do and why you believe what you believe.

It is important for you to understand that there are no wrong answers. The answers are yours and yours alone. I can guarantee that if I read the answers of one hundred people, no two would be exactly alike, and some would be completely contradictory. This is good. You are who you are, and you believe what you believe. Your passions and beliefs are yours, and you have specific reasons why you believe what you do. You act because something inside you compels you to. That call to action is strong within you, but could be nonexistent to someone who you care deeply about. This does not make it right or wrong; it makes it YOURS. Your POWERFUL PERSONAL BRAND is built upon your history, your experiences, your frame of reference, your upbringing, your relationships, your hobbies, and so on. No one else has the exact same life as you, and that is what makes you unique and interesting.

Embrace it! Own it! Celebrate it!

People are drawn to you because of who you are, not because you are a carbon copy of them. People want to experience things vicariously and being around people with different viewpoints and experiences allows them to do that. Be that person! Do not be afraid to be who you are and think the way you think. You may not be liked or loved by everyone; truthfully, no one is. However, by being you, you allow for those who do find you interesting and valuable to have a richer life because of knowing you. Do not rob people of this by playing it safe. Embrace your uniqueness, celebrate your passions and live your life with purpose.

So, I ask the question, who are you?

CHAPTER THIRTY-ONE

JAE M. RANG
PRESIDENT
JAE ASSOCIATED LTD.

1. **What is your definition of a POWERFUL PERSONAL BRAND?**

Everyone has a brand whether they realize it or not. Your values, your ethics and your goals all contribute to what you show the world who you are. A POWERFUL PERSONAL BRAND comes from identifying your strengths and then focusing on what you do really well to serve humankind. A POWERFUL PERSONAL BRAND is authentic, brings out the best in you and others.

2. **How has your POWERFUL PERSONAL BRAND allowed you to gain success in your industry?**

I've had my personality profile done several times over the years and the results are always the same: I'm an inspiring motivator. I am motivated and inspired myself to be the best person I can be with the gifts and tools I've received and can acquire. I've translated this concept into corporate branding and approach those clients the same way. I have written three books – one about the promotional marketing industry, one to offer branding tips, and one as a personal development tool to encourage people to create original thought. They're all an extension of my brand and desire to support personal and corporate growth.

3. **What advice would you give to those looking to create their own POWERFUL PERSONAL BRAND?**

   Take the time for self-discovery, to understand your own unique abilities and passions and focus on being even better at those gifts and skills. Create a sentence that describes who you are and why you do what you do. My mission is "To be a catalyst for positive change and inspired growth" and my branding statements are born from that.

4. **How do you perceive having a POWERFUL PERSONAL BRAND helps someone either secure a job or advance within a company?**

   I always say, "A little clarity goes a long way." When you're clear on who you are and how you want to serve, it makes it very easy for anyone to support you. The dilemma with many is that they are not clear on who they are. They may be clear on who they WANT to be but their actions are not in alignment with their intentions. Congruency is key. Identify your values and be true to yourself. Life will be both fun and easy and you'll attract all the right people. **Succeed deliberately!**

CHAPTER THIRTY-TWO

NOW HERE ARE SOME TIPS ON HOW TO APPLY WHAT YOU HAVE LEARNED

The key to a POWERFUL PERSONAL BRAND is being able to communicate it consistently. Understanding your value is worthless if you cannot articulate it to others in a meaningful way. So, now that you have made the effort and taken the time to understand who you are, what you do, why you do it, and your value in the world, it is time to let the world in on your little secret.

The first thing anyone has to do when developing their brand is to go out and get a great set of photos taken. Do not go cheap, and do not just get one that makes you look like you just got a shot for your passport picture. Look through people's LinkedIn, Facebook, or other social media feeds and find pictures with personality. Find pictures that are warm and engaging, and then narrow it down to people that live in your geographic area.

Once you have done that, reach out to them, find out who their photographer was, and then reach out again. Find someone who can bring out your true personality. Be bold, be unique, but more importantly, be you. Get pictures of you sitting, standing, facing different directions, happy, sad, serious, and silly. The reason for this is, though you are going to use one shot consistently across the banners of all your social media feeds, you will want the others to use at various times for various projects. Trust me: Having multiple headshots is always an asset.

Now, let me take a step back. Consistency of image across platforms? Why, you are asking? So there is no doubt it is you when people are looking for you. If your Facebook, Twitter, LinkedIn, Instagram, Snapchat, or whatever images are different, people will question whether it is even you, and therefore, it leads to brand confusion. This is something you just do not want to have.

As well, the personal vision statement you have been working on needs to be consistent everywhere. If it is not, then it is not your personal vision statement. Between your image shot and your personal vision statement, this is a major way to create consistency across platforms and let people understand who you are and what you do, no matter where they find you. It is a sense of professionalism, and people will acknowledge this and be drawn to it.

The next thing you need to do to maintain a POW-ERFUL PERSONAL BRAND is to find a voice. Understand what you speak on and what you do not. Understand what your point of view is and how you feel you can engage with people best to get your point of view across. It is all about consistency. Image and voice need to work together to allow people to have a clear picture of who you are, what you believe, and what your value is to them. Without that, there is confusion, and confusion leads to an inconsistent brand. Many people have never been hired, promoted, or considered for contracts because of the inconsistency of their brand.

Think about it! If you are applying for a position that you really want and someone checks out your social media feeds and the image that is portrayed is of you as a partier and a drunkard, how quickly do you think they are going to hire you? The same can be said for a promotion. If you have a reputation of being someone who talks ill of people, either in the office, or online, or worse yet, speaks ill of the company you work for, how amenable do you think that company is going to be to offering you a promotion?

This does not just go on inside an office. As someone trying to sell a product or service to a potential client, if they cannot trust you, why should they buy from you? That trust is part of your POWERFUL PERSONAL BRAND. People Google people. They check who you are on LinkedIn, Twitter, Facebook, and a variety of other platforms. They ask people who should know you, or know of you, what you are like and they form opinions of you before you even walk into the room. This is reality today. If you are not consistent, whether it is online, offline, in person, on the phone, or just in public, people will not know who you really are and with that your personal brand is tainted. Take the time and Google yourself, regularly, and understand that what you see, others do as well. Remember, I told you that you have a brand whether you realize it or not!

LinkedIn groups are a great place, if they are the right group, to develop and perfect this voice. Find topics that resonate with you, listen, observe, and then engage. Give people reason to see your arguments are valid and that your opinion matters. Do not be afraid to be controversial, IF you can back up your arguments. No one cares about another "like" on social media; they want people with opinions and voices of their own.

SOME THINGS BEAR REPEATING:

When you are developing your online voice, find articles online and share them with your followers, but never do so without adding an opinion as to why you are sharing it. It is your voice, in front of a well-written article, that will compel your followers to read it. Statements such as "I just read this article in Inc. magazine that talks about the lack of leadership in America today and it made me think as to whether people are embracing their personal brands

. . . what do you think?" will get much better readership than just sharing an article with no thought before it.

Engage with people on social media. Do not just hit the "like" or "heart" buttons! LEAVE A COMMENT! Give an opinion as to why you thought someone's thoughts were valid and interesting. Ask them a question about why they thought a certain way, or challenge their beliefs if you can back up your opinion. Having an opinion and voicing it is a key factor in developing your POWERFUL PERSONAL BRAND.

Create your own content. Whether it is written or video-based, create collateral that is yours. I write for magazines, have a weekly podcast, write a monthly newsletter, and I am constantly writing posts on social media. Not only are these seen by people on the mediums I engage in, but they are constantly being crawled by Google and Bing. Key words create hits on people's searches, and you want those searches to come back to you and not your competition.

Speak when you can. I do not care if you get paid for it or not; find ways to speak in public. It boosts your confidence, gives you ways to solidify your ideas, and allows people to see a more dynamic version of you. I speak whenever and wherever possible. Most of the time now I get paid for it, but a lot of times I do not and that is okay as well. If you do not want to speak in public, find podcasts or webcasts you can speak on. The great thing about doing this is that it is more content that you can post on your social media feeds and website, and all of it tracks back to you. There are thousands of podcasters out there always looking for new content. Provide them with something of value that will benefit their listeners, and they will love to have you on their program.

To summarize, a POWERFUL PERSONAL BRAND comes from purposeful consistency. It is the art of having a voice that allows you to speak as an expert within a narrow focus to a specific audience. You will never be an expert in everything, nor will you be perceived as valuable to everyone you meet, but that does not matter.

What matters is that you are valuable to people who need what you have to offer. Being the expert for people whose problems you can solve and stress you can reduce is an amazing person to be. Being the person who can solve problems and explain complex ideas in a simple and straightforward manner makes you valuable to them, and that is the key to having a POWERFUL PERSONAL BRAND. Understand who you are, understand who you are not, who you can help, and who you cannot, and communicate your value through both language and actions consistently.

So, what have you learned about yourself?

_____

_____

_____

_____

_____

_____

_____

_____

_____

_____

_____

_____

_____

_____

_____

_____

_____

_____

_____

_____

CHAPTER THIRTY-THREE

ALWAYS HAVE A STORY TO TELL

I cannot begin to tell you how important having stories to tell is in developing and maintaining your personal brand. We all learn from stories and we remember them. Your brand stories give people mental hooks as to why they should think of you when they need whatever you can offer them.

What do I mean by that? You need to have stories that illustrate who you are, what you do, why you do it, and the value that you provide. You need to paint a visual picture of your value in the eyes of those who you wish to influence. For example "Tell me a little bit about yourself" is something that I hear at least once a week. People want to know something about the people they do business with. Having that information in a story format allows you to easily recall it, tell it, and have it be engaging and coherent every time that you tell it. Otherwise, you are stammering for an answer, and that impresses no one. It is not about telling people your life story, unless they ask you for it; it is about having a few salient points at your fingertips that tell people who you are and what you do.

For example: I have been living here in Vancouver now most of my life. I have traveled pretty much halfway around the world, lived overseas, but Vancouver has always been home. I have been married for about 21 years now and have one son in high school. He is way brighter than I am . . . then again, so is my wife. I work with clients to help them tell compelling stories and engage their audiences in meaningful ways. What about you?

It is short, and to the point, but it is more than just work-related. It has a human factor to it and gives people reason to ask more questions.

The key to POWERFUL PERSONAL BRAND stories is that they have to be authentic. They have to be in your voice and come naturally to you. They need to entice your audience to want to know more and not be so long that they become distracting.

Tailor your story to your audience. Ask them about themselves first, actively listen, and find out what their passions are. Possibly you will find something that you both have in common like cooking, golf, or tango dancing. Who knows? But if you listen, you will have a better chance of relating to them on their level. It is not as much about what they say, but how they say it. If they are soft spoken, do not be loud and boisterous. If they do not share an enormous amount of detail, be succinct. If they are animated, you know it is ok to be the same, if that is part of your personality. Be curious, watch, listen, observe body language and intonation. All these will give you hints as to the style and mannerisms of the person you are talking to, and knowing those behaviors will allow you to engage in a way that is not going to be perceived as threatening or boorish.

Here is an example: I lived in Israel for three years. Israelis have a much different sense of personal body space than North Americans do. People stand much closer, and they are far more animated in their conversation style. Conversations can get loud, without being confrontational, and people use their hands to express opinions. After three years of living overseas, I had become very accustomed to that style of conversation and the mannerisms that go with it. As you might imagine, the first number of people who encountered me upon my return found me extremely forward, boisterous, rude (because of some of the hand gestures used), and overall not someone they wanted to be around. It took a close friend to mention this to me, and for me to take a step back and realize the differences in culture and communication. Once I understood this and changed my mannerisms to reflect those of the people around me, trust levels increased, people liked being around me much more, and my opinion was deemed valuable. I tell this not only to illustrate a point about culture and body language, but also to point out that you now know more about me, based upon the story I told.

163

Here is some space to put down your story ideas:

CHAPTER THIRTY-FOUR

TIM MCCLURE
PRESIDENT
TIM MCCLURE AND PARTNERS

1. **What is your definition of a POWERFUL PERSONAL BRAND?**

A great personal brand defines exactly who you are – not what friends and family think of you, not what sugar-coated marketing material and fancy brochures say, but who you REALLY are!

Can it change over time? Sure, we should all want to evolve, be willing to continue learning, and be open to change. Change is inevitable, but life can be pretty amazing if we are wide open to it! That said, we need to have that foundation that is solid, demonstrates consistency and focuses on perfecting the basics – things that you can always go back to in challenging times, or when momentum swings happen in your life...and they will happen!

167

For example, in a sport like hockey, great coaches will make sure that their teams get back to the basics of the game when they are going through a slump – skating harder and with more fluidity, passing with more crispness and accuracy, and shooting the puck on net.

In our personal and professional life, perfecting the basics means doing the simple things like being on time, listening, being prepared, and focusing on being present.

2. **How has your POWERFUL PERSONAL BRAND allowed you to gain success in your industry?**

You have to determine what your ideal outcome is...where you want to go. Without that clarity, you stand no chance of getting there. Only you can decide this!

I have always built my entire career and personal life around transparency.

I wrote a quote that says: "Integrity...you either have it or you don't! There is no in-between." I really believe that and live that every day. I don't "try" to live it...I DO live it.

Early in my career, my first mentor was a man named Bill Christian; he was a Founder of Christian Hockey Sticks. I will always remember him saying, "Timmy, just do what you say you will do!" That always stuck with me, and I carried that on to my days as Senior Vice President, Starter and in my role as Vice President, Luxottica.

168

I am not perfect by any means, but people that know me, in business or my personal life, realize that I can be counted on. Today, that is a very important quality to have at any level, and at any stage of a person's career.

3. **What advice would you give to those looking to create their own POWERFUL PERSONAL BRAND?**

First and foremost, define what brings you gratification and happiness.

Know what YOU want to do, not what others think you should do! Put all of your focus onto finding that place, and do not base what brings you happiness solely on money. Making a lot of money but missing out on what feeds your creativity and passion is a mistake, and eventually it will reflect on your performance. This will impact your personal brand.

Secondly, learn to focus. Be present. It is possible to hear every word, yet miss the message completely. The biggest distraction from building your personal brand and the momentum to get your message out is to continually chase "shiny objects"! This is so important.

Find your lane and excel at it; do not get caught up spreading your focus over too many things. If you hope to excel at anything, do not try to be an expert at everything.

When building your personal brand, seek counsel from others who have had success, but who have also experienced failure and made mistakes along their path. Experience does not just mean putting in time; it is what people have done with that time, and how they have used their experience going forward.

Preparation helps to breed positive results; positive results breeds confidence, and confidence puts you into a place where you never talk yourself out of being great!

Finally, if you want to get results fast, get to the point and do not be afraid to ask for what you want! People respond better to those who are straight with them. Do it with consistency, and you will gain the respect that will build your stable of people who want to listen.

4. **How do you perceive having a POWERFUL PERSONAL BRAND helps someone either secure a job or advance within a company?**

Your personal brand is everything in today's business environment!

If you have built a reputation as being consistent, confident, and someone who can be counted on, this is worth so much to an employer! It can earn you much more room to be creative and gain more responsibility.

People want to be around other people who help create momentum. Be that person.

If you show that you are teachable, committed to learning, and always trying to grow through taking additional courses, following influencers that inspire you, yet demonstrate an ability to step up and offer creative, thoughtful input, you will develop a reputation of someone that is also a "go-to" person in the organization. That can help you excel in your position, and your confidence can soar!

CHAPTER THIRTY-FIVE

SO, NOW WHAT?

Simple: Get out there and live your life. Be the most interesting you that you can be. Do not try to be someone else, because people will see right through that and your personal brand will be worthless. Stand up and articulate your beliefs, help others to be better, and create opportunities whenever and wherever possible for greatness to happen.

Celebrate the uniqueness of you and be curious about the uniqueness of others. Find out what you like, or dislike about other people and figure out why. Remember, it is not the what that is the most important part of this whole exercise. What I like or dislike about someone or something is easy to determine and articulate; why I like or dislike someone or something is so much harder to put into words coherently. Be curious about the world around you and take the time to figure out what you can learn to make a better you. We can all improve, we can all learn, and we can all use this knowledge to help us make POWERFUL PERSONAL BRANDS.

What is your action plan?

CHAPTER THIRTY-SIX

BEN BAKER
PRESIDENT
YOUR BRAND MARKETING

1. What is your definition of a POWERFUL PERSONAL BRAND?

A POWERFUL PERSONAL BRAND is who you are at your core. It is what you believe and how you demonstrate and articulate those beliefs to others. But that is only half of it. It is also defined by how those you interact with perceive, internalize, and communicate that POWERFUL PERSONAL BRAND to others. I define a POWERFUL PERSONAL BRAND as one where those who engage with it find it valuable. The actions and the words of the POWERFUL PERSONAL BRAND are consistent, and they inspire those who engage with those with POWERFUL PERSONAL BRANDS to be better versions of themselves.

2. **How has your POWERFUL PERSONAL BRAND allowed you to gain success in your industry?**

My POWERFUL PERSONAL BRAND has allowed me to have the confidence to go after my goals. It has allowed me to communicate effectively and demonstrate to others my value to them. It has allowed me the ability to succeed, on my terms, and help me make the world around me a better place to be.

3. **What advice would you give to those looking to create their own POWERFUL PERSONAL BRAND?**

A POWERFUL PERSONAL BRAND is as much about understanding and listening to others as it is about you. The more you can earn the trust of others, the more valuable they will find your thoughts and actions and be willing to follow your lead.

4. **How do you perceive having a POWERFUL PERSONAL BRAND helps someone either secure a job or advance within a company?**

A POWERFUL PERSONAL BRAND helps people succeed in either securing work, or advancing within a company, by demonstrating courage, tenacity, forethought, and drive. It is the confidence that you exude and the ability to effectively communicate your value and trustworthiness that draws people to you and makes them advocates for your success. Be the person people want to emulate. Say what you mean and do what you say you will do. Be the person people can trust to do the right thing and to tell the truth. Your brand is your reputation and your reputation is your brand, and both are earned through hard work and consistency.

EPILOGUE

Now is the time for you to go back and answer the questions I have posed to you. Take the time to question your beliefs and ask yourself why you think the way you do. In the end, either you will solidify your beliefs or be on the path to discovering new and interesting things about yourself. Either way, you win!

As I have mentioned throughout this book, we all have POWERFUL PERSONAL BRANDS, and whether we understand them or not is up to us. It is up to every one of us to explore who we are, what we do, why we do it, the people we wish to influence, and why they should care. It is about investing the time and effort to explore what we believe in and what we are willing to fight against. It is about codifying that belief structure and being able to articulate it in a way that is comfortable to us and compelling to others.

Never think this is an easy process or something that you can do overnight. Building a POWERFUL PERSONAL BRAND is something that takes time, effort, reflection, and asking a lot of hard and sometimes scary questions about yourself.

As you age and your situation in life changes, so will your personal brand. You will go from being single to dating, to engaged, to married, to being a parent, to being a grandparent, to being a grieving child, and a thousand other things within a lifetime. Realize that your personal brand will change based on those situations that come before you. Understand that life is change. It is understanding the changes and incorporating the lessons learned from those experiences that allow us to grow and make our personal brand more powerful.

The best thing you can do to develop your POWERFUL PERSONAL BRAND is to go out and live it. Be yourself, and communicate and demonstrate what you believe in. Be authentically you!

Enjoy the journey, embrace it, learn from it, and use it for good.

May you learn from your past to create opportunities for your future.

To your success.

Ben Baker

*Truthfully, it does not matter
if you perceive the glass as being half full or
half empty.
. . . The most important thing to remember is
. . . that it is refillable.*

– Ben Baker

ABOUT THE AUTHOR

I help brands tell engaging stories that compel their customers to take action.

I am a father, a husband, a believer in community, and a passionate teller of the stories of brands. As the founder of Your Brand Marketing and the YourLIVING-Brand.live show, I work hand in hand with my clients to understand what makes them special and unique in a crowded space. It is by understanding the nuances of a brand, the special things they do that others do not, that unique stories can be told and audiences engaged.

I am available to consult, provide workshops, and speak on brand, message, market, vision, and value. My goal is always to tell the right story, to the right people, in the right way, so that the intended audience listens, understands, internalizes, engages, and is motivated towards action.